Mo on the Nantahala

Micheal Rivers

ISBN-13: 978-1466345980

ISBN-10: 1466345985

For Belva
My good friend for a lifetime

CONTENTS

PROLOGUE

There are those who believe that true love can never die. It is neither an impossible affair of the heart nor is it just the words of poets wooing your soul. The tale of Edward Caulfield stands as a testament of the love he held in his heart for a woman he was never allowed to grow old with.

Though the trials of life are never easy, someone to stand with you and help you with your burdens is one of the true essences of living. It is well that two should join together to face life as friends as well as lovers.

Through the centuries those who knew the power of prose have placed before us stories of those who never again gave their heart to another after time has taken the one they loved. It is my hope you will have all the treasures in life that a true heart can bear

Chapter One

In the silence of midnight, memories stirred as leaves on the wind. By the banks of the Nantahala River, an old man stood watching the pale blue light of a full moon caress the gently flowing water. Nineteen ninety-five was another year when he would stand during the full of the moon and be here watching, waiting, not ending his vigil until the wee hours of the morning gave way to false dawn. Edward Caulfield was here to witness the Lady of Nantahala. It was here he would try to discover the true identity of this fine lady who had caused such a stir within those who came to walk by the river. In his heart he knew it was his Celia, it could be no other, and still he had to see her to truly believe.

The shadows of the hills and mountains surrounding him whispered her name gently. He yearned for the sight of her, just a glance to soothe the pain deep within his heart. A beautiful lady dressed for the ball waltzed alone upon these waters, waiting for her love to join her. She never smiled as she twirled and danced lightly through the mist swirling upon the dark waters. Some would say they had seen her eyes. It was true enough there was certain sadness there not to be denied.

Many years ago Celia had vowed to Edward on her deathbed they would be together again, never to part for eternity. He believed her and clung to every word she whispered as she passed from this life.

Edward Caulfield was not a man to believe in just anything! The words that escaped the lips of his beloved wife on the night she left him were forever in his ears. The very sound was the same, neither wavering nor changing for a second. He believed in her and cherished every word she had spoken to him for the few years they had been married. If indeed it was his beloved Celia, why then had she allowed herself to be seen by others and not by the man who still loved her with all of his heart?

The years had taken their toll, and with it came the time when Edward had to make a decision. He knew he was old and needed the things all men do when they can no longer continue for themselves. He made the decision to move from his home and reside in a smaller house. The thought of having another woman in the house he and Celia had made their home was almost blasphemous in his eyes.

Edward moved into a small bungalow closer to town, nearer to the local physician. Dr. Wayne Early had been his friend for many years, and when the time was upon him, Edward took Wayne's advice and hired a housekeeper.

The search for just the right person to accompany him in his old age did not take very long. He knew very well whom he would ask to stay with him and promptly made her an offer. With little or no hesitation, Betty Curtis made arrangements to move into his new home that very day. He gave her a generous space of her own and a substantial salary to entice her not to leave him until it was time for him to die. All of this was really not necessary for the number of years they had known each other. She was happy to be there for him, just as he had been there for her and her husband while he was still living.

The house he and Celia had built was two miles from the bungalow he now called home. Each day he would walk the distance back to his old house and sit beneath the cooling shade of the ancient oak trees, listening to the river roll by beyond the slope of the land, recalling every minute he could of his life with Celia.

Cool summer evenings brought back the memories of seeing Celia standing close by her flower garden waiting for him to come home from work. He could almost smell the aroma of fresh-baked bread she had made for his supper. Just a spark of the life he had once had was enough to please him and carry him forward to the next day. Should he close his eyes and concentrate hard enough, he could still bring back the lilt of her voice as she greeted him.

There was a time when he would go beyond the front doors of the two-story house and wander through the rooms, doing everything possible to recall the things that happened in them. He would run his fingers slowly across the stucco walls, barely touching them while listening to old familiar creaks of the floorboards. Now, he was content to just sit and look at the house. The white paint that once covered the exterior was all but gone, and so too the shutters that once kept out the foul winds of winter. It hurt him to see some of the windows had been shattered by children coming here to play. He wasn't angry, yet he had overheard children calling his home "the haunted house by the river." This did disturb him somewhat, for he and Celia had wanted children badly and had hoped they would love the house as much as they did. He wanted everyone to love this house as they had. These words coming from the mouths of youths were heartbreaking to him.

Edward had made his way to the center of town early one summer evening in 1976 to attend the annual fireworks display. He sat smiling and laughing with his friends as they shared a bottle of the local talent's best moonshine. The evening wore on, and after the fireworks were done, the men still sat and talked late into the night. This was the night Edward first heard of the Lady of Nantahala. A stranger in the small group of men told the story of his experience, and seemed not to notice when the men of the town tried to change the subject. Edward knew from the man's description of her it could only be Celia. His heart froze in his chest as he listened to the man's words. She was nothing more than something to amuse him. The other men whom he had called friends for so many years had seen the same apparition, and yet they never said anything to him. It was more than obvious by the hesitation in their answers to the stranger's questions that they were well aware of everything the man had witnessed. They had recognized her and didn't want to hurt Edward by talking about what they had seen. It was in their eyes—yes, it was in their eyes!

After the night of the celebration, Edward found it difficult to look into his friends' faces when he met them on the street. It was not because they did not tell him of what they had seen, but rather he felt he may say some small something that may give away the secret that he had never been allowed to see the Lady of Nantahala.

In the spring of 1995 Edward began to notice a young woman walking the narrow gravel path by the riverbed. He could glimpse her as she would find a spot closest to the tiny whirlpool beneath a small stand of river bamboo. There she would sit surrounded by the small ferns growing beside the banks, sometimes with what appeared to be a journal of some sort. On other occasions she would just sit and watch the water flowing lazily by with a book open in her lap. He was curious as to why one so young would prefer to be alone in a place of such beauty. It was not for him to question, and he would turn back to his thoughts and daydream of days long past. For three years, each and every summer Edward watched for her, knowing she would come, knowing she would return to watch the waters of the Nantahala. For three years she never failed him.

Edward sat resting in his chair beneath the familiar oaks of his home, smoking his pipe and humming an old tune long forgotten by many. He grinned slyly to himself as he heard the low crunch of gravel beneath someone's shoes. She had returned again. Slowly he turned his head to assure himself that it was her and she was alone. All of these years and he still did not know her name. Yet he felt as though he knew her very well. He knew the sound of her steps, the sound of her voice when she hummed bits of melodies to herself. Edward felt a strange comfort when she was near. She never intruded upon him, and always left a lingering scent of herself that was quite pleasing.

Minutes passed and Edward lost sight of her. Had she decided not to stay on a day as beautiful as this? A twinge of disappointment touched him at the thought of this being so. Edward drew in lightly on his pipe, gripping the bowl in his left hand as he turned his head to search for her.

"Good morning!" a cheery voice called to him. "I hope I didn't startle you," the young woman said with a grin.

Edward turned quickly toward the voice almost directly behind him. "Not at all, young lady. I didn't see you coming up behind me." He chuckled.

The young woman smiled slightly. "Yes, you are right. It isn't proper to sneak up behind someone and speak. But I couldn't knock first."

Edward laughed heartily. "Ah yes, youth and a sense of humor. What more can someone ask for?"

Her face reddened slightly. "I suppose I really should introduce myself. I have been coming here for a few years now and have just discovered from the grocer today the property belongs to you. That is if you are Mr. Caulfield?"

Edward nodded politely and assured her he indeed was Edward Caulfield.

"I know this is not the right time, but may I have your permission to come and sit by the river?" she asked pensively.

Edward grinned. "You have been coming here for three years during the summer months and sometimes in the fall. Who did you think I was?"

The young woman looked away, not sure how to answer him. "I wasn't sure, but still it has taken me this long to find out."

Edward stood from his chair and leaned heavily on his cane. He turned from her and gazed steadily at the old house before him. Cocking his head slightly to one side, he stared grimly at her. The young woman stepped back slightly, as if she was in fear of a physical reprisal for venturing onto his property. Suddenly Edward broke into a huge grin.

"There is something you have to do before you are allowed to come here, now that I am fully aware of your coming and going. I will not tolerate you being here otherwise."

The young woman stiffened slightly. Her voice held a sharp edge. "And what would that be?"

Edward laughed heartily. "Take it easy, rest yourself, and tell me your name so I do not have to refer to you as 'young woman.'"

With a release of her pent-up breath, she smiled. "I'm sorry. I should have introduced myself long ago."

Edward eased back into his chair, looking up into her face. "Yes, that would have been the proper thing to do."

"My name is Leonora. All of my family calls me Lena. But I usually answer to almost anything," she said.

Edward laid his pipe on the small wooden table by his chair and pulled his hat lower over his eyes. "What name would you like for me to call you?"

Lena opened her mouth slightly as if to speak, and still she found she could not. She had no answer to the question he had put before her.

Edward chuckled. "I'm sorry, but it sounded to me as though you may have a name you prefer other than Lena or Leonora. Am I correct in this assumption?"

Lena blushed. "My dad had a pet name for me that I liked very much, but it wouldn't sound the same coming from someone else."

Edward nodded again and turned away from her, easing into his chair. "Okay, I'll call you Lena and we'll go from there. You can call me Ed, but only when you arc using my name."

Lena giggled like a small child. It was nice to meet someone with such a whimsical sense of humor.

Edward pointed to the chair next to him and smiled. "You can sit here for a while if you wish. You are welcome here anytime. I will warn you though: sometimes I am not all that social. Sometimes, at my age, I have a tendency to go through quiet spells."

Lena glanced around her and decided she did not want to sit in the chair next to him. With a flourish, she almost made a ceremony of taking her seat in the grass beneath the shade of the trees. Edward nodded to himself. This was a fine thing. She had a mind of her own; he liked that very much. Something about her made him curious, very curious. Her smile bordered on being forced, and although she was friendly, there was still a little something there that convinced him all was not what it seemed.

"Lena, would you care for something to drink? I understand it is a bit early, but I have never been one to stand on ceremony. I always bring a little something to ease the tensions of the day when I am here," he said.

She recognized the twinkle in his old eyes immediately. "Are you trying to tell me you tend to imbibe on pleasant days like today?"

Edward laughed. "If that's the way you want to look at it, then yes, I do. Sometimes I imbibe to the point I have to get a nap before I start for home."

Lena glanced toward the old house and then back to Edward. "I think that would be wonderful! I can't remember the last time I sat in such a place and enjoyed a good drink."

Reaching behind him, Edward pulled a bottle of Nantahala's finest from a small wicker basket covered with a bright red cloth. "I don't have any glasses, so you'll have to do it the old-fashioned way. Sorry about that."

Lena watched intently as he uncorked the bottle. The liquid inside gave the illusion of being more clear than the spring water she had become accustomed to in the years she had been making her treks to these mountains. After her long slim fingers wrapped themselves around the bottle, she then brought it just below her nose to take in the aroma of it. To her surprise there was not the strong alcohol aroma she was expecting. Instead there was the lightest scent of rose petals. "Is that rose petals I smell?"

Edward grinned. "Yes, it is. The man who makes this uses just a little to take the edge off. You'll get used to it, and you don't taste anything odd when you drink it. It makes it very pleasant, if I do say so myself! I first started getting this from him back around 1940 or so. He is a little younger than I am, so I am not worried about running out of it."

He watched her as she laughed at his words. She had a pleasant laugh. He hated women who laughed and sounded as though they were horses or some other such nonsense. The slight wrinkle about her eyes gave way to genuine mirth when she laughed. Edward's thoughts began to run.

The women he was acquainted with today usually wore jeans and T-shirts when they were out taking their walks. This lady was different. She dressed neatly in a blouse of some sort, which he had no name for, and a long skirt. Her manner of dress reminded him of a Gypsy in so many ways. She was fair-skinned with long, slim arms and delicate hands. She walked with a grace not at all usual for the ladies of today. To Edward, he would be willing to bet her mother had done everything possible to attend to the lessons of bringing up a lady, and nothing less would be acceptable.

He was right in his assumption. Her mother had been adamant about the virtues of being a lady at all times. It was Lena who had been adamant about the fact that even a lady should be able to have fun without being a prude. In the end she had won the skirmish with her mother, but at a terrible price. They were never close to each other again, nor did her mother wish to discuss any aspect of her life. These were the minor points Edward gleaned from her life in the following weeks they spent in each other's company, and Lena was quick to divert any conversation that would lead to anything concerning her present state of mind.

Edward thought of Celia and wondered if they had been granted the gift of children, would a daughter have been much like Lena? He wanted to believe she would have been. What could have been on this child's mind to weigh so heavily? She came to his home to take refuge from life, and he was willing to give her the peace she craved within her, if only for a while.

It was another beautiful afternoon when Edward met Lena once again beneath the shade of the aging oak tree to sit and talk. His thoughts had lingered on the things she had told him during their discussions about life. He had added up everything he knew of her and found there was something amiss. Something did not ring true with her.

Edward reached down and picked up a small twig, twisting it slowly in his large hands. Such a small thing, and still by doing so he could bring his thoughts to bear with a certain clarity. He missed working with his hands. There were many things he longed to do once more, and yet he knew it was not to be. Celia would have understood and helped him through these times of not knowing what to do with himself; she would have understood all too well.

Lena glanced over at him, cocking her head ever so slightly. The sun on her hair reminded Edward of his sister whom he had lost so long ago. Where had time taken him? So many things reminded him of days long past. The memories stood in his shadows only to appear at what he deemed to be the most inappropriate times.

"If my old memory serves me correctly, you have hair the same color as my sister when she was about your age," he said.

Before she could comment, he turned and stared down the path, seeing everything, seeing nothing but the ghosts of old friends long gone from his life.

Without looking back into her face, he began to speak. "Lena, you come and sit by this river every day. For a few weeks now we have been talking, and yes, we have talked of pleasant things and a few old times here and there. But I want to ask you something, if you don't mind?"

She stared down at her feet. She was already uncomfortable with the direction she felt the conversation was headed. Lena looked back up into his eyes, brushing the hair back that had fallen about her face. "Edward, I feel as though you are about to ask me something I may not want to answer right now. Are you?"

Pulling the brim of his hat back down over his eyes, he slid back farther into his chair. "I considered asking you many things over the time you have been coming here, and sometimes I didn't really care one way or another. Today I have a lot on my mind. It seems like such a heavy load to bear, and it all concerns you. I have become really attached to your visits. You would be surprised at the amount of time I spend thinking about coming back here and listening to you. Don't take it the wrong way with the affection part. You have listened to my ramblings for quite a while now. I want you to know how much I appreciate you and your company."

Lena leaned back against the trunk of the ancient oak and stared up through the leaves as she spoke gently to him. "I enjoy coming here, and I have enjoyed talking with you, Edward. At least when I am here I have no doubts about what will happen. Sometimes there are small surprises, but they are always pleasant. Case in point: that wonderful ham and cheese you brought. I'll pry the secret of where those came from out of you before I have to leave here."

She laughed easily and pressed the back of her head gently against the tree.

Edward stood to his feet. Reaching back behind the chair, he picked up the bottle and turned it to his lips. The liquid went down smoothly, and it was comforting and warmed him to his bones. This comforted him, feeling somewhat easier about what he needed to ask her.

"Lena, I have watched you for a long while, and I know there is something weighing heavily on your mind. I'm telling you as your friend: if I can help you, please let me know."

"Edward, I have nothing bothering me that you can help with. Besides, what makes you think I do?"

Leaning against the cool bark of the trunk of the tree, he looked down at her. "I may be old, but I am far from stupid. Your face is like a road map to misery. Your smile is full of tears and your walk tells me you dread the thoughts of the future. I'm not so senile that I imagine things. Fact of the matter is, my doctor says I'm mentally sharper than most people he knows. He can't find his butt with both hands, but he still swears I am not losing my faculties."

"If you are aware of so many things, why don't you tell me what you know?" she asked angrily.

Edward held up his hands in mock defense. "I am saying these things as your friend, someone who wants to help you."

Lena just sat and stared at him, saying nothing.

Edward gave a low whistle in exasperation. "A young woman such as yourself doesn't come to a place like this as much as you do without something being amiss. I believe things are not quite what they seem."

Lena jumped to her feet, her tiny fists clenched tightly to her side. "What would you know about me? I go and do as I please, and nobody tells me what to do."

Edward grimaced. He could see the slight traces of tears running down her cheeks. "I'm sorry if I brought up a bad subject. I know you are married because you talk in your sleep while napping. There is a problem with your home life, or you would not come here alone year after year. I am not condemning you for anything. I just want to know if I can be of some help to you. I will make a bargain with you. We will exchange the stories of our lives. This way I may be able to help you in some small way. That includes all of the ham and cheese you can ask for."

Lena sat down heavily. There seemed to be very little leeway around this subject. She knew it would have to come to light sooner than later, yet she wasn't prepared to deal with it even now with Edward.

Edward's voice was close to a whisper. "It will be all right, Lena. When you are ready, I will be here for you."

Without another word, Edward gathered his things and headed for the gravel path toward home. Each step took him farther from her, with the knowledge that he may never be able to help relieve the burden she seemed to carry. Sometimes it was better to lay the seed of hope before someone and let them decide if it is the best for them. He prayed she would change her mind and let him try to help her. After today, the chances of never seeing Lena again were entirely possible. There was never any intention of hurting her or making her angry. But he had no doubt in his mind he had spoken too soon and too much for his own good. He slowed his pace as he glanced back over his shoulder to see her still beneath the shade of the oak, her head buried in her hands and crying. Edward felt a chill run through his bones as he noticed the slight shudder of her shoulders as she wept. He never meant to hurt her. He only wanted for her the things he would have done for a daughter of his own.

Days turned to weeks and still Lena had not returned to his old home to visit. Edward shakily made his way down by the banks of the river to see if she had returned for even a moment to sit by the river as she had done before they met. There was never a sign of anyone except the prints of his own shoes in the mud.

Heartbroken with the thought he had driven away his friend by prying into her life, Edward came home early this day. The front door of his bungalow seemed dreary. The place had never taken on a life of its own as it should have. A home should be vibrant and welcoming to everyone, yet this house bored him to tears. Betty, his housekeeper, had asked him several years ago about planting flowers and giving the house some life. Edward had agreed readily enough and the flowers were beautiful, and yet something always felt as though a very special thing was missing. He knew what was missing. Nothing gathered the light of life as his Celia had. She opened the heavens for him with just her smile, a smile he could not live without.

Edward reached and removed his battered hat from his head, and tossed it on the couch just as Betty popped into the hallway.

Betty was by no means a small woman. Edward had hired her because she loved to laugh. He needed that in his life, and she obliged with nearly every breath she took. "Mr. Edward, you are home mighty early today. Did your friend not come to visit?"

Edward smiled a faint little smile and sat down in his favorite chair. He preferred to have his chair here regardless of the scolding he always received from Betty concerning napping by the open window. Slowly he raised his hand in defense from the words he knew would be coming from her. "Before you say anything, Betty, I am not moving this chair, and it would be to your benefit if you didn't either. As far as my friend is concerned, no, she was not at the house today. I expect she has better things to do than listen to the rambling of an old fart like me. I came home because I am just a little tired today, and thought I might sit and read the paper before midnight for a change. Are you happy now, or should I write all this down for later consumption by you?"

Betty curled her lip. "My, aren't we just a little snappy today! I was just trying to make conversation and you turn it into a novel. It'll never be a bestseller at the rate you are going, that's for sure."

Betty fussed with the pillows on the sofa and made her rounds to each and every little porcelain figure in the room as she tried to talk to him. "Sometimes I think you are in love with that little girl. You act like such a schoolboy whenever you have spent the day with her. You ought to be ashamed of yourself, a man your age trying to act like you are twenty again."

Edward sat watching her, his finger lying pressed along the side of his nose, his eyes twinkling with laughter. He dared not laugh out loud for fear he would make her angry. He never wanted to make her angry, but he dearly loved to tease her and watch her go off like a rocket.

"Betty, are you sure you're not jealous? I could have sworn I saw a little green flash just then. Maybe me and you can run off to Tennessee and raise fishing worms or something. Then on our afternoons off we can fool around down by the dump."

"Sometimes I think you just want to try to make me mad, old man. Well, I got news for you: it *ain't* going to work. Not now. Not ten years from now, so be satisfied and get on with it. Your supper will be ready about six, so don't you get it in your head you're going to sleep and let it get cold before you sit down to eat."

Edward snickered under his breath as she stomped out of the room. It was a game to him to try to stop the way of giggling she had after the end of a sentence. A game he enjoyed immensely. Tonight, it wasn't nearly as much fun. He felt genuinely tired. A strange feeling of weakness about his limbs and muscles worried him to no end. Shaking his head to clear his mind, he simply passed it off as the effects of old age.

The evening newspaper lay unopened in his lap. There seemed to be little or no interest today in what he called the *Daily Rambler*. Local events no longer interested him, and the thought of reading the classified ads drove him from his chair. Edward headed for the kitchen with intentions of getting a large handful of Betty's homemade cookies. He didn't really care that he was not supposed to eat sweets. Nor did it matter to him that the wrath of Betty would rain down upon his shoulders for eating them. All that concerned him at that moment was the delightful taste of something special for a change.

Betty eyed him closely as he reached into the cookie jar and withdrew a large handful of the molasses cookies she had baked. Edward caught her watching from the corner of his eye and placed half of his hoard of sweet heaven back into the jar. Much like a small child, he went and sat silently at the table, and waited for what Betty was going to say.

"Mr. Edward, you know Dr. Early said you cain't have no cookies and such, it'll kill you and you know it!"

Edward laughed easily. "Yeah, that's what he said, but I don't see him here right now, and he'll never know 'less you tell him."

Betty chuckled. "I ought to tell him for sure, but then again I don't see how it's right for a grown man to be refused something he likes. If I ever get to your age, I reckon they'll be tellin' me the same thing. Make you a deal, Edward. You put back a few more of those cookies, and I'll make you a cake that won't hurt you so much. I found a recipe for a fine cake that is just for folks that cain't eat much sugar."

Edward nodded his agreement and placed a few more of the cookies back into the jar, and the rest except for onc hc slid neatly into his pocket for later.

Betty reached into the cabinet and pulled down the plates for their supper. As she placed his plate gently down on the table in front of him, she grinned broadly. "Before you leave this kitchen, I want you to put those cookies in your pocket back in the jar, or there won't be any cake!"

Edward heard her laughing as she walked away to get the silverware. He could swear she had eyes in the back of her head and a nose like a bloodhound. Edward stomped out of the kitchen, swearing under his breath. "Seems like I just cannot get past that damn woman no matter how hard I try!"

Betty called back over her shoulder. "No, you cain't get past me, and don't slam that door on your way out!"

Edward slammed the door with all his might, jarring it on its hinges.

Betty laughed. "Foolish old man, just like I wouldn't know that's what he was gonna do anyway."

During the months of summer and on into the fall of the year, Edward enjoyed his evenings sitting on the front porch and rocking slowly back and forth in the rigid-back cane rocker Betty and his friends had given him for his seventy-fifth birthday. It was here he liked to smoke his pipe and gather his thoughts while gazing deep into the pool of stars above him.

There were times when his thoughts returned to the days of his youth, remembering with great clarity the feelings that came upon him as he lay back beneath this same southern sky and held his beloved wife close to his side. Edward chuckled beneath his breath. *So many years have passed, and still it seems like just hours ago.*

Hearing the groan of the rusted hinges of the screen door behind him, Edward turned to see Betty coming out of the door. He watched her as she moved slowly by him and sat herself down on the porch swing, her feet dangling with the tips of her toes barely reaching the pine boarding that covered the porch floor. He had to admit that it was nice to have someone to talk to at times. Still, there were many nights not a single word passed between them.

Betty cleared her throat loudly. Edward cringed, wishing she would just come out with what she had to say instead of making that God-awful noise before she spoke her mind.

"Mr. Edward, I do wish you would let me know where you are during the day just in case something should happen to you."

Edward laughed. "You worry too much. Besides, you generally know where I am at any time of the day. Sometimes a man needs to have some time for himself, unless you don't approve of it," he said with a devilish grin.

Betty's face flushed a crimson red. "You know what I am talking about, you old coot! Last Tuesday, you were up the street to see your lawyer friend and you fell down comin' out of his office. Just suppose you would have hurt yourself and nobody was there to see. You could lie there and die and nobody know it."

"There was nothing to it, Betty. I slipped and went down on one knee, not even so much as a scratch. I'm careful enough for both of us."

Betty looked off toward the church, admiring the way the brightly painted steeple stood against the night sky. For her, it was a beacon for all to see the house of God.

"Mr. Edward, I generally do all your errands for you. Was there something you needed to do so bad that you couldn't even let me know where you were going to be?"

Edward pulled his pipe from the corner of his mouth and leaned heavily on the arm of the chair, looking deep into her eyes and ignoring her last comment. "Betty, how long have we known each other?"

She laughed heartily. "I first met you in the spring of '51. You were the boss down at the sawmill. That was the same day my husband lost his leg, if I recall. You were mighty good to both of us, and I appreciate it."

Edward still looked steadily into her eyes. "I did go see my lawyer. Betty, when you moved in here, I promised you I would see to it that you never lacked for anything as long as you stayed here. You have been faithful with your end of the bargain, and I appreciate it very much. You're a good friend and companion."

Betty interjected, "What are you trying to say? Are you gonna let me go after all this time?"

Edward laughed. "No, you don't have to worry about anything like that. But I will tell you what I was doing at the lawyer's office. I will be eighty-six years old this Friday, and I know I am not a young man any longer. I have started preparing a little better for when my time comes to leave God's green earth. I know you have a daughter in Atlanta and a son in Texas. Over the years I have found out they are not as dependable as I would like for them to be when it comes down to your welfare. That's why I went to the lawyer's office. When I'm gone, this house will belong to you free and clear for as long as you want it or as long as you live. Either way, it will be yours. The only thing you will have to do is keep up the taxes on it."

Betty sat straight up, almost in shock. "Mr. Edward, I can't accept this house from you. My daughter will take me in, I'm sure."

Edward's voice came through the night air calm and clear. "You won't have to second-guess whether she will or won't, and you can have the privacy you need. You don't have a choice in the matter. The title to the house has already been placed in your name, and you will have to sign it after I am dead."The silence that followed was unsettling to the both of them.

Betty gathered herself and went back into the house. Edward could swear he saw tears in her eyes as she passed him by. In his mind she deserved it. She had worked hard all her life and had little or nothing to show for it.

He knew he had no family to speak of to leave his worldly possessions to, and the few he did have deserved nothing of the fruits he had harvested for his labors. Celia would have approved. He well knew she would have been happy about his decision. Smiling to himself, he stood from his chair and nodded at the stars above him. *Good night, Celia. Tomorrow is another day, and I must get up early. Never forget how much I love you*

Chapter Two

The weeks went slowly by, and he had not heard a word from his friend. He feared he had seen the last of her.

Edward awoke early on a Wednesday morning. He lay in his bed looking out of his window, watching a fat robin feeding her young in the nest. He smiled to himself, thinking about how some things in the world never changed.

A slight noise coming from the kitchen brought him back to reality. Betty was already up getting breakfast ready, and the familiar sounds of pans rattling brought him to his feet. It was hell getting old. Every morning his body got up with him one piece at the time. Within a few minutes, his feet felt as though they belonged to the rest of his body and he headed for his morning shower.

His shower finished, he toweled himself dry and looked into the mirror. He had considered growing a beard, but with the shape of his face, he felt that would be a mistake.

Entering the kitchen, he spied Betty bending over the oven door and removing a tray of fresh biscuits. Edward smiled. "Good Lord, woman, do you have to wear that frock so early in the morning? You didn't wear that out there to get the paper, did you?" He knew this would get her wound up for the day. Betty prided herself in trying to look nice, but the temptation was too great for him.

Betty stood erect and placed the hot pan on the stovetop. Placing her hand on her hip, she shook the spatula toward him. "Be careful, old man, the last thing a feller ever wants to do is make the cook mad when you're low on toilet paper! Now sit down and eat, before I throw it out."

Edward snickered to himself and sat down in his favorite chair. He ate his breakfast like a man on a mission. Downing his coffee in two swallows, he rose from his chair and grabbed his cane from beside the door. Betty looked surprised. "Where are you off to in such a hurry?"

Looking back over his shoulder, he told her he was going down by the river and would be back for lunch. Betty raced for the door. "Take your hat, it's gonna get hot 'fore you know it."

As he placed the hat on his head and headed down the front steps, Betty closed the door. "Crazy old man is gonna forget where he is one of these days, and I'll have to go get him for sure."

The walk to his old house by the river was always pleasant. This time of morning the birds sang in the trees, and the sound of the water rolling by always brought a smile to his face. He stepped to the edge of the riverbank and watched the water rolling over the rocks. When he was a child, the sight was a fascination to him; it seemed that feeling never had left.

Edward hung his head, lost in thought for a few seconds. This was the same spot he had asked Celia if she would marry him. The memory of the moment was imprinted on his mind for all time. Closing his eyes, he could almost hear her voice telling him it was all she ever wanted. Reaching the yard, he pulled a worn Barlow knife from his pocket and cut a few of the fresh roses Celia had planted there. The aroma reminded him so much of her and her loving smile.

Edward finished the short walk to his house and stood on the front porch. It was hard to keep from recalling the many times he had placed his hand on the door handle and walked into a memory.

The interior of the house was cool, almost damp. He stood in the foyer and noticed the fine sheen of dust starting to cover the old furniture and all that surrounded it. Edward made a mental note to ask Betty if she would help him get the house back into order when the weather changed. She couldn't work as well as she could before because of an onset of arthritis in her hands and back. It was easy to understand and sympathize with her. After all, he knew the feeling well.

A few of the windows had been broken by vandals, and yet they did not enter the old house. Edward was surprised someone had not tried to move in without permission. Maybe Celia had placed her mark upon the house and life respected that. Edward chuckled to himself. No, he had just been lucky, and that was all.

The sheets covering all the furniture had helped to preserve it, and yet time was taking its toll on his memories. Walking into the living room, Edward raised one of the windows to allow the air to circulate around the room. He turned away from the open window and pulled one of the yellowing sheets from a wing-backed chair he had always favored at the end of the day. The royal-blue covering had not faded as much as the other furniture had, and he was grateful. It seemed to ease his mind to be able to sit in this chair by the window and reminisce.

Edward pulled his battered hat from his graying head and placed it neatly on the floor beside his chair. With little forethought, he began to speak aloud as if all was well with him.

"Celia, I haven't forgotten today is our anniversary. I hope you don't mind that I cut a few roses from your garden. I put them here on the table. Dear Lord, I wish I could see you again. I'm so lonesome."

Edward raised his head, cocking his chin toward the mantel of the fireplace. He could have sworn he had heard the whisper of someone calling his name. He lay back in the old chair, with his head resting on the cushion. The voice came again much stronger and clearer through the house. He sat erect and looked about him. He would swear the voice was Celia's.

"Is that you, Celia?" he called out.

"Celia, please talk to me." Edward's voice sounded weak and almost childlike as it echoed through the room. He had spoken with her in this very room years after she had left him. He yearned for every second he could hear her voice.

Celia's voice came to him once more. It felt as though she was all around him and nowhere at the same time. "Edward, I am here."

Edward raised himself shakily from the chair and stood nearly in the center of the room. "Where are you, Celia? I want to see you."

The voice continued to feel as though it was all around him. "Edward, I can't do that. Hear my words and be well with them. It is all I can do."

Edward was on the verge of tears. "Never forget I love you, Celia."

Celia's voice crooned close by his ear. "I know, Edward."

Edward felt a gentle touch to his cheek and knew she was no longer near him. He sat back into the chair for a while longer and wished he could have had more time with her. At times he looked forward to his own death, knowing he would be with her again.

Edward walked to the window and closed it tightly to keep out the elements. The simple act of re-covering the chair brought him pain, but it must be done. He walked back through the front door and locked it behind him.

As he stepped from the porch, he heard Celia's voice again. "Don't worry, Edward, she will be back."

Edward wheeled about, hoping to catch a glimpse of Celia. The only sight he was able to capture was a small ball of light disappearing into the house through the door. The message was clear to him. Celia was letting him know Lena would return and they could talk as they did before. With a smile and a spring in his step, he headed for home.

Betty sat on the porch swing and nodded to Edward as he mounted the front steps. Betty cleared her throat gently and grinned. "So, how is Miss Celia today?"

Edward looked at her with mild surprise. "You know Celia is dead, Betty. Why do you do that to me?"

Betty rocked the swing gently and looked Edward in the eyes. "You men are all alike. You think you are the only one things happen to. I have known for years you have been talking to her. You talk in your sleep. You cain't make up things like that, not even in your sleep, old man. I also know today was your anniversary." Betty arose from the swing and started for the door. "Your lunch is ready." Without turning toward him, she said lightly over her shoulder, "I've been talking to my old man for years, and you went to his funeral. Seen him once or twice too!"

Edward couldn't believe his ears. She had never said anything like that before. It made him wonder what else she knew about him.

They ate their lunch in silence. This felt like a blessing for Edward, for fear of having to tell Betty what he felt deep inside.

The mail usually arrived around eleven every morning. Edward relished going through his mail, but as of late the joy was gone. Today there was a letter awaiting him with unfamiliar handwriting. There was no return address and it was postmarked from nearby. He opened the envelope carefully and pulled two sheets of perfume-scented stationery from it.

As he began to read, he realized the letter was from Lena. She apologized to him for getting angry and walking out. She wanted to know if the deal was still intact after her imprudent behavior. She made known to him she was fully aware the deal would expose everything. If he agreed, she would meet him by the river on Thursday morning. The postscript was written with a flourish: *Your friends were quick to give me your address.*

Edward closed the envelope and stuck the contents in his pocket.

Betty was watching him from the kitchen and saw the look of pleasure on his face. It was good to see something had sparked a bit of life back into a man by giving him something to look forward to.

Edward called out, "Betty, can I ask a favor of you?"

Betty never turned but kept cleaning the kitchen table. "Are you trying to tell me there will be lunch for two tomorrow? If you are, I already been to the store and got that ham you love so good."

Edward shook his head. "Are you a magician or a psychic? Sometimes I think you know too much for your own good."

Betty laughed loudly. "It ain't that, I just know you too good. That young lady won't gonna go away that easy. From what you told me, you and her is all there is. You don't fool nobody. If you really think you can help her, I say try it with all you got."

"Thank you, Betty. You are a blessing most of the time. The other half is too nosey for your own good." Edward walked back out of the house and headed for his workshop behind the garage. He stayed until the sun was just setting behind the mountaintops.

The night passed quickly, and Edward rose early to be able to try and get to the riverbank before his guest. Betty had breakfast ready and declared she would be gone for the day shopping. She advised Edward to take it easy today and not push himself too hard.

Usually Edward questioned her shopping days, but not today. He looked forward to talking with Lena. Maybe Celia would be close by and help him get Lena back on track with a better life. It would be a life filled with happiness instead of misery.

As he rounded the curve close to his favorite tree, he spied Lena already there waiting for him. She had a look about her that bordered embarrassment. The day would go well, he knew it in his heart.

Without a word, she walked up to him and took the basket from his withered hand. She looked down and noticed Edward still wore his wedding ring.

Lena and Edward walked back to the tree in silence. Neither of them knew where to begin. Edward sat heavily down into the chair and grinned. "Good to see you again. I'm glad you changed your mind."

Chapter Three

Lena looked down at her feet. "It wasn't an easy decision. The alternative had even less appeal."

Edward was puzzled. "Did something happen since the last time we spoke?"

"Actually, many things have happened. I also had to come to some decisions concerning my life that aren't very pleasant," she stated very frankly.

"Maybe this is a good thing. It could give us a starting point for our deal," he said.

Lena laughed. "You are not going to get away that easy, Edward. I am going make you the guinea pig for the first round."

Edward smiled to himself. The tension had already begun to ease between them. "That sounds fair. Be forewarned: I may fall asleep in the middle of a sentence. Where would you like me to start?"

Lena leaned back in her chair, resting comfortably. "I think you should start as a young boy. That would be interesting. It would also tell me what kind of man you are."

"I believe that is fair enough." He nodded his agreement. Without hesitation, he began his tale. "If I am correct, this is the year 1998. If my eyes don't deceive me, it looks a lot like spring, with the heat coming early this year."

Lena nodded. "Please continue."

"My parents came to this country as immigrants. If I remember correctly, my father was from Cornwall, and my mother was from Lancashire. Both were hard-nosed English with the old-school flair. My grandfather also lived with us until about 1920. He died in his sleep. I am eighty-six years old, and I hope to see eighty-seven. Two of my brothers were born in England, and the other three of the children were born here. The old home site is another county over from here."

Lena interjected, "Don't get ahead of yourself and leave out something important to me."

Edward laughed. "I will do my best, but memory is one thing I seem short on lately. Not to mention whether or not the memories are correct."

Lena plucked a Mason jar from the picnic basket and swallowed a large gulp of Nantahala's finest whiskey. "Okay, please continue. How many sisters and how many brothers?"

Edward flinched when he saw her drink the whiskey as if it were nothing but water. "I had two sisters and two brothers. All of them are dead and gone now. I am the last of the Caulfields as far as I know. None of my brothers or sisters had children of their own."

Edward's thoughts drifted as far back as his mind permitted. There were many things that would come to him later, but age played tricks with his memory. "My father was very strict, as well as my mother. In later years I realized he had a temper he either could not or would not control. On occasion, I saw him hit my mother. Sometimes he would leave bruises on her face. She made her excuses and stayed away from town on those days. It was a sad time, and a child can do nothing but stay quiet and away from the danger.

"Don't get me wrong. He provided for us better than most, and he rarely showed his anger to any of the family. He drank a bit, and I guess he had the right. I don't believe he was an alcoholic. At the same time, he drank his share and then some. He believed in teaching his sons to be men. The girls were just girls, and he paid little attention to them. When you were big and old enough, you began to work doing whatever you could to help. He said it wasn't a point of money. It was the way to learn your way in the world. He believed a working man was an honest man. He believed it so firmly that he worked himself into his grave before his time."

"What kind of work did your father do? Did he have a trade?" she asked.

"Yes, he did have a trade. He was a woodcarver in England, as his father before him. They produced some of the finest furniture I have ever seen. When he came to the States, my father and grandfather opened a sawmill. They cut firewood, lumber for houses, and hardwoods for furniture.

There was a large shop behind the mill where my father and grandfather built furniture. They would do it all for the right price. I started working in the sawmill when I was twelve. My brothers and I worked the mill twelve hours a day, six days a week, unless we were at school. Before you ask, no, we did not have a choice. My father said one day I would thank him." Edward laughed aloud.

Lena leaned forward slightly. "Do you regret those days?"

Edward thought for a second. "You cannot regret something you have always been taught to be right. If it is the only life you know, it can't be regretted because you do not know any different. I was taken to work in the furniture shop while my brothers worked in the mill. I remember my grandfather had a habit of looking at our hands. I heard him tell my father I had the hands of a craftsman and he would be obliged if I was to be taken into the furniture shop and taught the trade. My eldest brother was very intelligent, but my father would never let him speak of any of his ideas. This caused a lot of friction within the family."

"I feel like a child should be able to express his feelings and ideas. But who am I? I had the same problem. Please continue." Lena stood now, leaning against the tree and staring at the waters of the river as they passed lazily by them.

Edward drank lightly from his cup and stretched in his chair. "I had a good childhood, I think. We fished and hunted. This was recreation as well as providing more food for the table. I learned more from my father and the men who worked for him than most men would learn in colleges today. I never tasted war as my brothers did, and I have no regrets. I saw firsthand what it had done to them. They were never the same after they returned home. It was as if the flame of life had been extinguished within their souls."

"What of your mother? You say very little about her," Lena said pensively.

Edward turned slightly away and stared over the mountain as he spoke of her. "She lived a hard life, as far as I remember. I rarely saw her when she wasn't working and caring for us. I only saw her smile once in my entire life. That was the day my youngest sister was born. My mother was not a large woman. She had a lot of internal strength. I saw pictures of her when she was a young girl in England. No doubt she could have had her pick of any man. She fell in love with my father, and the rest is history. She was forty-six when she was found in the laundry shed. The doctor said she had a hemorrhage of the brain. According to him, she was dead before she ever hit the floor. Her hands were rough and calloused, but she always smelled like a tropical flower. My father was never the same after her death. He spent every minute he could at the mill. I feel like he just didn't want to come home."

"Who was taking care of you after she died?" she asked.

"My mother's sister came to stay with us. I never liked her. There are people in this world that have never harmed you and still you don't like them. She was one of those people for me. I stayed at the mill with my father just to avoid her."

Lena said nothing and walked away from Edward to stand in the sun for a moment. Edward was curious why Lena would want to know these things. He had made a deal and must stick with it if he was ever going to be able to help her. She seemed to be in deep thought as he watched her pace in the sunlight. Occasionally she would look back toward the mountains as if she had too much on her mind.

He was sure she was more interested in his life with Celia than his childhood. First things first, as they say. Time has a strange way of passing for a man. Life is and always will be the same for everyone in some aspects. Mankind does not change, nor do his actions when it comes down to how he lives his life. The advances that are made, such as technology and other modern conveniences, steadily change. But the mind of man can only teach what he has learned from others. It is how you use that knowledge that will decide who you are.

Edward never understood many things until late in life. He had no children to leave his legacy of knowledge and advice to. Possibly Lena may learn some sparse bit of experience from his life to leave to someone else. It would be a legacy from an old man that would carry over the ages to those who would care to listen.

Lena returned to her chair, and they ate their lunch in silence beneath the shade of the old oak. Edward was just finishing the last bite of his sandwich when Lena looked straight into his eyes. "Do you regret telling me anything so far?"

Edward hesitated. "I did at first, but now I'm glad I told you. I had not thought of my mother in years. I regret I never had children of my own at times because of her. There are people who know how to share their love without ever saying a word. She loved us, of that I have no doubt. I wonder now if she was just telling us in her own way how much. I wish things could have been easier for her."

Lena chuckled. "Both sides of life can be seen if you look hard enough. My mother said life was not meant to be easy for women, it was just the other side of the coin nobody wants to see."

"Do you think that's true?" Edward asked.

"I think life is what you make it to be. There comes a time when you have to stand up for yourself or be trampled by the herd." Lena grinned broadly.

"I do believe you have had a revelation as of late. Which brings us back to you. It is your turn to talk to me," he said.

Lena exhaled heavily and turned to face him. "I was born the princess in the family. Being the only child is not what some people would call fun. It has all the advantages of the best clothes and toys, but you get pretty lonesome for someone to talk with. Mother and father are notorious for having rods up their backsides. Levity is crude and meant for the lower classes in their eyes. My father made his fortune in the steel industry, while the queen mother doted over the latest fashions from Paris. The hair, makeup, and clothing had to be perfect at all times. When my father went into politics, he won a seat in the Senate without trying very hard. It was nice to have friends in all the right places.

"When I was eleven, we moved into a house you could get lost in very easily. However, the queen mother said it would do until my father ran for president. That part still has not happened. I'm sure my mother will never rest until she resides in the White House. I pity the hired help if she ever moves in. My father never spent much time with me, but when he did, I could see a man that deserved more than my mother for a partner in life.

"My father called me his Lotus after the lotus flower of Japan. He always called me that with a great amount of affection in his voice. I was never allowed to get dirty nor have friends over unless mother approved of their families. From early on, I had to attend etiquette schools in various countries and practice being a total snob.

"I can speak six languages fluently, among all the other treasures education can bestow upon you. The main fault I have in life, according to my mother, is the penchant for being crude. I love fried-egg sandwiches and that makes her stomach roll at the very thought."

Edward laughed uproariously. "So you are telling me your mother hates you because you are normal. Personally, I can't see you being a snob. I am sure you are very lovely when dressed for the ball. That doesn't make you a member of the elite. The elite are a different breed than what your mother's idea seems to be. Some of the men I have a great deal of respect for do not have two nickels to rub together. The mark of distinction belongs in the actions of the heart."

Lena nodded. "I totally agree. I have no idea where she obtained her ideas from. She was not born into a rich family. Neither was my father. With his success in life he has paid the price of living with a woman who could not survive without a maid.

"At sixteen, my coming-out party was just like anything else I received from her. None of my friends were allowed to be there. Instead, she invited all the kids from the other senators' families. She picked my escort for me. His father was the richest man in politics by her standards. I took one look at him and almost lost my lunch. He smelled like old gravy and his tuxedo fit like a clown suit. Everyone knew he was spoiled beyond belief, and there was never a time when his mother didn't take orders from him. I suspect his tuxedo was fitted during one of his tantrums. I was embarrassed to death as my mother stood by my father cackling about what a wonderful couple we were. A year later I burned the pictures while she was touring Greece."

Edward could not stop laughing. "Another case in point where money was the ruler of all that is holy for her, I suppose. When did the tide turn for you?"

Lena grimaced. "I'm not so sure it ever has."

"Why do you say so?" Edward frowned.

"My mother still drags me to hear the screeching of the opera and demands my appearance at parties I do not want to attend."

Edward shook his head, not understanding why Lena's mother would not let her live her own life.

"We had a private theater in our house for watching movies. I never saw the inside of a movie theater until I came here. The best part of the movie was the thought I chose it for myself. When I am here, I never worry about something being said about my clothing or hair. It is a feeling I could learn to live with very easily."

"What is stopping you from becoming the person you want to be?" Edward asked.

Lena ignored his question and walked over to the river. She stood without saying a word. When she turned, she told Edward it was time for her to go home. She still had some things to pick up before dark. Edward nodded and watched her stroll down the path toward town. It was obvious his last question had struck a nerve. Tomorrow he would try to get her to tell him the reason. For now, it would have to wait.

Edward gathered his basket and cane. He stood staring at his house, wondering what this time would be like if Celia was here. The path seemed longer each time he came here. How soon, he wondered, before he would not be able to see his house anymore?

It was just after dark when Edward mounted the steps to his cottage. Betty opened the screen door and asked him if he was all right. He admitted he was very tired but well. Betty was quick to tell him that she was just leaving the house to go and find him. Normally Edward would have had a fast retort. He just smiled a shy smile and said he thought he may go to bed early tonight.

Betty was well aware this was out of his character. She went to the bathroom medicine cabinet to check his medications. He had taken them on schedule just as he had told her. She thought she would have a word with his doctor as soon as she could and let him know about the changes in Edward.

She slept lightly that night. Betty continued to check on Edward while he was sleeping to assure herself all was well.

When he came to breakfast the following morning, he grinned slyly at her. "Good morning, Mother Hen."

Betty folded the dish towel and glared at him. "Mother Hen, is it now? You were awake last night for sure. Just like a man—play possum when somebody gets to worry 'bout you."

Edward grinned as he started to eat his sausage. "Betty, I appreciate you worrying now and then. I was all right. I was just a little tired from my walk home, and that's all."

Betty sat down at the table and shook her fist at him. "Old man, you are gonna be the death of me. You didn't eat your supper, and you nearly had to drag yourself into the yard. That's right, I was watchin' you. You get yourself home at a decent hour and take care of yourself. You act like I'll always be here. Well, it ain't so. Now you go get your clothes on, and we'll go from there."

Betty made her way to the sink, ignoring Edward for the rest of the time he sat at the table. Without a word, he left the table and headed for his bedroom to get dressed for the day.

Edward hummed an old tune as he dressed himself. There would be some extra time today before he made his trek to the river's edge. Lena had an appointment she could not change and would be later than usual. With this in mind, he decided to go to the coffee shop downtown and visit with a couple of friends. They were always trading the latest gossip in the county and were usually right about every subject that was broached.

Edward reached the old shop just in time to see Freddy Wilkes going in through the exit door. His eyes had failed him long ago and he couldn't see a train sitting ten feet from him. Edward heard him exclaim as he nearly toppled a lady leaving the coffee shop. Edward laughed aloud and grabbed the door just in the nick of time. "You'll have to excuse my friend, young lady; he thought he was headed for the restroom."

Freddy turned at the sound of Edward's voice and sneered. "Very funny, Caulfield, did you think of that by yourself?"

Edward tipped his hat to the lady as she bustled by and then grinned at Freddy. "Freddy, I would suggest you get your bottles checked. Your vision is getting worse every day."

Freddy smirked and slammed himself down in the booth closest to the door. The coffee shop was not dark, but it gave the illusion of a subtle shade permeating the atmosphere. The ancient ceiling fans turned above them so slowly you would wonder if it was just a breeze turning them or the dance of the dead. The faded red leather seats sank down to where you felt the springs pounding your butt each time you made the slightest move. Edward hated that feeling. He often wondered if the old booth seats were going to fall to the floor when he reached for the sugar.

A waitress walked over to their booth and inquired as to what she could get for them this fine morning. Her smile was infectious, and Edward wished for just a few seconds that he felt as well as she looked. Freddy cocked his head and ordered coffee. His thick glasses were covered with a film of greasy fingerprints. One wondered if he saw her at all. His crooked smile looked almost evil in the dim lighting of the old shop.

As she walked away to gather their order, Edward turned back to his old friend. "How is life treating you these days, Freddy?"

"Not bad, been better. I heard you have gotten a little sugar on the side these days. The word is you have been seeing that little girl from Clark's Ridge. I saw her once or twice. She is a fine catch for an old fart like you," Freddy stated flatly. His voice was bordering on jealousy.

Edward shook his head and looked up to see the waitress bringing their coffees. She placed the cups in front of them and asked if there would be anything else today. Edward thanked her and told her he would let her know.

Turning back to Freddy, he spoke to him matter-of-factly. "You have been listening to gossip for so long you don't even bother to find out what is true any longer."

Freddy grinned. "So, you are going to deny it? She has been meeting you down by the river for a few years now. If that is a lie, everybody seems to know it."

Edward almost spit his coffee across the table. "Where did you hear that piece of stupidity from?"

"It's what everybody says. Old lady Saunder told me about it yesterday. She said she saw you two down by the river curled up with a picnic basket." Freddy took a deep swallow of his coffee.

Edward grimaced, and his thoughts ran wild with what all of the busybodies were speculating. He leaned back in the booth and glared at his old friend. "There is nothing going on with me and the girl. I do appreciate that all of you think I am still capable of chasing skirts."

Freddy grabbed the sugar dispenser and added two more heaping spoonfuls to his coffee. "I am not so sure of anything anymore. I only know what everybody is saying."

"Who is 'everybody,' Freddy?" Edward asked slyly.

Freddy shrugged and grabbed his cup with both hands. "Everybody is everybody, Edward. It is that simple."

Edward finished his coffee and started to rise. "This has been pleasant, Freddy, but I have to go. Good to see you again."

Freddy just nodded and reached again for the sugar dispenser. Edward was just outside of the door when he spied Betty coming down the street. He stepped back into the shadows for a moment and watched as she looked up and down the street. He was sure she was searching for him. He also knew she would try to herd him into the doctor's office. That wasn't going to happen if it was his choice.

Betty disappeared into the door of the barbershop, and Edward slipped quietly down the sidewalk in the opposite direction. Once he felt safe from her prying eyes, he grinned and did a little dance step. It felt like being a kid again and dodging your parents.

He stopped for a few moments to rest at the tiny park by the traffic circle. Sitting on the dark green bench by the Civil War memorial, he casually glanced around the little town. He tried to remember where everything was when he was a child growing up here. The furniture store was now a boutique for the yuppies who had come to perch like vultures. Most of them considered everyone here to be beneath them. They never stopped to consider when they needed help it was always the locals that came to their rescue.

The building next to the boutique had been empty for a very long time. It was once the ice-cream parlor and drugstore. Some of the remnants of the advertising specials still hung haphazardly in the dusty windows.

Looking at the empty sidewalks brought a bit of sadness to his heart. There was a time these streets were teeming with life. Everybody had a smile and a kind word for one another. Strangers were greeted in the same manner neighbors. It all seemed now like a place out of step with the rest of the nation. Edward glanced to his left and saw a teenager weaving his way up the street. His shirt displayed a huge swastika. His unkempt appearance was an abomination in Edward's eyes. Edward pumped up his chest in disgust. *In my day, I would kick your skinny ass all over the street for wearing that. Be thankful I am too old to stomp that shirt off your back. Damn kids have no sense of right and wrong these days!*

The kid walked past Edward and nodded his shaved head as he strolled by. Edward never acknowledged his presence. Shaking his head in disgust, Edward rose to his feet and headed for the river. Times had changed, but the old still clung to the things they knew in their world. History is history, and time marches on. What was once an abomination to the world was now a simple fad to those unaware of the history behind the symbol of hate that was an atrocity to man. He had failed to stop and think this young man came from a different place in time and probably knew nothing of the symbol's origin.

Chapter Four

Bypassing his usual seat beneath the tree, Edward walked around to the back of his old home. He stood inspecting the wood and windows for a moment. He knew he should get the windows repaired, and soon. Two of the windows on the second floor were completely broken out. In his diligence to watch the house and catch up on old memories, he had inadvertently neglected the things that were necessary to keep the house alive.

He always kept a pen and a small writing pad in his pocket. This was a habit his father had taught him early in his youth. It was his conviction that the pad and pen was a necessary tool for everyday life. Edward had to admit the notepad had saved him from some very large mistakes over the years.

Peering through the dusty windows, he could barely see the kitchen. This would not do at all. What would Celia say if she were here? Reaching for his pad, he made another note to have all of these things taken care of. He knew he was still capable of taking care of part of the details, but not all.

Leaving the back porch, he rounded the corner and saw Lena standing in the yard. She grinned broadly. "I see the master of the house is on an inspection tour."

Edward waved a hello and walked over to her. "As a matter of fact, I am. I have neglected my duties and must correct my lack of action." He then gave a slight bow, spreading his arms in mock homage to her. Lena curtsied and laughed. "It is so awfully difficult when a knight pays homage while sporting his cane," he said.

They both laughed and agreed to sit on the front steps of the house beside the rose bushes.

"Your rose bushes are very beautiful this year," she said.

Edward stared wistfully at the roses. "Celia planted those to decorate the yard a bit. These are actually wild roses I brought up from the gorge. At that time nobody cared what you took from the riverside. Now you might get two years in prison for it."

A silence fell between them for only an instant, each waiting for the other to speak. After the awkward moment had passed, Edward asked gently, "Where did you and your parents live?"

Lena sighed heavily. "I was born in Rhode Island and spent most of my years growing up in Virginia. The journey from there to here has been a long one."

"I see. Your parents traveled a great deal, did they not?" he asked.

"Yes, it was almost constant. New York, Philadelphia, Chicago, all of the major cities and around the world. Nonstop fun and frolic for all. It would have been nice if I would have been asked if I wanted to go instead of being dragged kicking and screaming every time." Lena looked away from Edward as though she had let him into her heart too fast.

"Don't take it so badly. You are a grown woman now and free to do as you please," he said.

Lena looked into his eyes as if he had lost his mind. Looking behind her, she asked Edward when he was going to give her a tour of the house. The only other person who had been in the house was Betty when he asked her to help him keep it clean.

Lena was young and did not quite understand why he had kept the house like a shrine for a woman who was dead. She was under the impression Edward and Celia were married for a very long time.

"Edward, how long were you and Celia married?" she asked.

Edward paused for only a second. "We were married three years, two weeks, and one day."

Lena exclaimed, "I thought you had lost her recently."

Edward's eyes appeared to be covered in a fine mist. "No, I lost my Celia a very long time ago. It is strange, but sometimes I feel like I never lost her. It is almost like she has taken a trip and I am waiting for her to come home again."

Lena folded her arm within his and whispered, "I am truly sorry for your loss."

Edward patted her arm gently and pulled away from her. "As you said, that was a lot of years ago, and it is something only I can deal with."

His answer baffled Lena. What was it he was trying to deal with? He said it as if a great battle was being fought within him.

Once more she tried to entice Edward to show her the house. It was to no avail. He was not ready for her to come into the house he and Celia had made their home. It was his sanctuary from the rest of the world outside. It was here he could be everything he wanted to be and bare his soul to the woman he still loved. It was difficult for others to understand the peace he found when he was alone in the house with the memories of Celia.

Lena smiled, trying to cheer Edward up a little. "Okay, I'll wait until you are ready. Then you can take me on the grand tour and tell me more about Celia and what your life was like here."

Edward finally gave in and agreed to think about letting her see the house. "I have a few things I want to do before I let you see the house. I hope you don't mind. If you were to go inside now, Celia would come back just to kick my behind for allowing guests inside while it's dirty."

Lena smiled sweetly. He still talked of Celia as if she were just down the street shopping somewhere. The years of listening to her father had made Lena more than a little observant of her surroundings. She was a great judge of character and noticed things others would dismiss. Edward always spoke of Celia to be among the living. He would readily admit Celia was dead, but she was always at his side. An enigma in the gray was what Lena considered him to be. There was no sense of being delusional concerning his character. How did Edward exist in two worlds without confusing them or the people who knew and loved him?

Lena lightly placed her head against Edward's shoulder and patted him gently on the arm. "How did you choose this piece of land for your house? What was the attraction?"

Edward's thoughts drifted back to when he first saw the property. "I was barely nineteen when I first truly saw this land for what it is. It was a small grassy meadow that held a certain magic for me. I sat by the river fishing where you used to go and sit with your thoughts. At that age I was just getting to know Celia, and I was so in love I could hardly wake up without her on my mind. I caught some beautiful trout that day and walked back up the hill to the path. I stood over there under the old oak and looked out over the meadow. Strangely enough, it felt as though it was already mine and waiting for me. I always wondered if a higher power chose this place for me."

Lena lifted her head from his shoulder and tried to envision what he may have seen in his mind. "This must have been a very pristine place at that time."

Edward grinned. "I would say it was the most peaceful place on earth. It still is for me."

It was not hard for anyone to notice the contentment of this old man whenever he spoke of his meadow. It was his refuge. This rang true with every breath he took. There were ghosts here to make his life more comfortable. The meadow fairly echoed with his memories of old friends, family, and most of all, his beloved Celia. Lena would have traded her soul for someone to love her as Edward still loved Celia.

Edward glanced down at his feet and started to speak. Softly at first, and then with conviction in his voice. "There are things you must remember, Lena. The old have lost much in this world.

"When you are young, you take many things for granted. Be it man or woman, the time will come when you will miss the taste of a true love's kiss. Within the eyes of the old are dead tales of dreams never spoiled by a spoken word. Life becomes filled with the illusions of things they have missed. In the same breath they have dwelled in the gardens of passion. A passion for life like no other but the old would know. It is as real as the wind blowing gently through the trees in the night. Often you will see the eyes of those on the verge of death gazing into the absolute. We will never know what they see, but the look of their eyes is without a doubt a subject for speculation. Reach out to the joys of life and caress them for all they are worth. Your kindness will one day return to you tenfold and bless you with the gifts life has to offer."

Lena listened to his every word intently. There was something in his voice that demanded all of her attention. The words so softly spoken came from his soul. She knew she had spent more days than she cared to remember hating everything and everybody close to her. Was it so clear to him the hatred she had for others in her life? The look in his eyes told Lena he saw her in a different light. For Edward, it was a light born to shine for others. She wished in her heart she could feel the same way. Why could she not see herself as Edward saw her?

Edward rose stiffly from the porch and stretched his long legs. "When you close your eyes, what do you see?"

Lena stared at him quizzically.

Edward smiled benignly. "Don't rush yourself. Give it some thought, and the answer will come to you." This being said, he walked away toward the river, leaving her questioning where he could be heading with a question that made little sense to her.

Lena watched Edward for a short time as he stood by the water's edge. She was unsure as to whether she wanted to venture to his side or be content to let him gather his thoughts. She decided on the latter and leaned back against the steps of the old house. The gentle mountain breeze embraced her. Lena closed her eyes and reveled in its soothing effect on her senses. Without opening her eyes, she knew when a small cloud had passed before the sun. Her heart felt lighter than it had in years. A great burden felt as though it was trying to remove itself from her very being.

Lena laughed gently as her thoughts darted from place to place. *Have I been so blind as not to see where life has taken me? I made my choices, and now I feel as though I knew nothing about what seems to be and what truly should be.*

Suddenly Lena opened her eyes and stared straight at Edward. He was still standing by the river's edge, but he was looking at her with a smile that almost took her breath. She could swear he had heard every thought passing through her mind. Tipping his hat to her, he picked up his basket and cane and left her without a word. She almost called out to him but realized she could not speak. She could only follow him with her eyes as he disappeared around the bend of the river's path.

Lena wrestled with the thoughts of returning to her cabin. It was indeed something to be proud of. It was also fast becoming a refuge for her. The cabin sat high upon the mountain with a view some would die for. There were days when she never noticed the view from her living room. It was just as if an artist had placed a panorama of someplace foreign to her across her windows. It brought no joy to her heart. It became a wanton feeling of loneliness in a crowded room.

When she finally arrived at her cabin door, the evening sun was just beginning to set behind the mountains. A myriad of colors gave way to a gathering of storm clouds on the horizon. She gathered her candles and oil lamp in anticipation of the coming rains. She lost her electrical power each time a storm appeared. A generator was a very nice convenience when the power was out, but she enjoyed the light of the candles while listening to the falling rain.

Shortly after midnight she retired to her bed, falling ever deeper into the lonely silence of the room. The slight tap of rain on the roof almost echoed through the room. It did not last for very long. Within the hour, a steady rain drummed across the rooftop and all around her. It was comforting and brought feelings of nostalgia. The sound of the rain was like an old friend coming to visit.

Sleep was not to come easily on this night. A nagging swirl of emotions clouded her mind. Against her better judgment, she decided she would call her home and wish her husband good night. If there was a small chance of saving her marriage, she would have to be the one to take the first step. He would not bow to apologizing for any of his actions toward her. This point had been made perfectly clear on too many occasions. In his mind, he was the king of the house and never wrong about anything!

Reaching for the phone, Lena picked up the receiver and began to dial. She hoped it was not too late to be calling. Glancing at her bedside clock, she saw it was approaching two in the morning. If calling late angered him, it would not be the first time.

The telephone rang several times before a voice came on the line. It was not her husband. The woman who answered the phone sounded a bit sleepy and breathless. "Hello."

Lena sat listening in silence. The woman spoke again more clearly. "Hello, who is calling please?"

In the background, Lena heard the shower being turned off and her husband talking from the bathroom. "Who's on the phone?"

The woman turned away from the receiver. "I don't know, they won't say anything. Should I hang up?"

Lena still sat in silence listening to them. Her husband's voice came on the line. He growled like a wounded bear. "Whoever this is, say something or hang up." A hesitation in his voice came through loud and clear. "Lena, is that you? If you are calling, I need to talk to you."

Lena eased the phone back into its cradle and climbed out of bed. The voice on the phone had been Susan's, his secretary. That would be one explanation she would love to hear! Not tonight though. No, it would have to be a time when she could think clearly. The phone had been answered in her bedroom. It was the only room in the house with an adjoining bath and a shower. Her rage was unabated at the very thought. Reaching out for the closest object to her, she grabbed her hairbrush and threw it across the room. The brush bounced off her dressing-table mirror and landed in a pile of glass shards. "Great, my husband has another woman in my bed, and I get seven years of bad luck!"

Throwing her hands in the air, she climbed back into bed and covered her head with the sheets.

Edward was experiencing his own miseries that same night. He was unable to sleep and found himself staring at the stars and dreaming of better days. The night air felt good to his aching bones. The sound of frogs croaking in the distance was a reminder of better times. Often as a child he had sat and listened to the frogs calling out in the night. His grandfather had told him the frogs were having a great debate. The debate would last until a king for the night was elected. Every night a new king was elected to rule for the next day. Being a child, he thought it was true.

Edward laughed at having been so naive. He had to admit it was a great story for a child to hear. His grandfather had a story for everything. While his father sat in silence, his grandfather smiled his toothless smile and gave you a reason for everything.

Hearing Betty rising from her bed, he returned to his room in silence. Sleep came to him easily this time, and he dreamed of running through the fields after a large hound he had used for hunting. It was just a dream, but for Edward it came to him when he needed to fill a hole in his memories.

Edward slept late into the morning. Betty did not awaken him. She wanted him to get some much-needed rest. When Edward was ready, he walked into the kitchen and found no sign of Betty at her usual station. He looked through the house, finding nothing to suggest she was at home. Grabbing his hat from the coat rack by the door, he stepped out onto the porch.

Betty sat grinning at him. "Did you sleep well?"

Edward grunted. "Yes, I did. It was nice to sleep in for a change. What are you dressed for? Did you have plans for the day?"

Betty stood from her seat. "You left your notepad in your britches pocket. I almost washed it. Anyway, I called Buck Queen and he'll be there at the house this afternoon to fix the windows. I got everything to clean the house with loaded in the car, and you are taking me to lunch."

Edward was dumbfounded. "Are you in hurry or what?"

Betty grinned again and handed him his cane. "You can sit wherever pleases you, and I'll get the house cleaned up. I don't want you in my way while I'm doing it. The diner has got baked chicken today. You like that, and so do I. If you can get to the car, we'll be on our way."

Edward just shook his head in amazement. It would have done little good to argue with her. It was just her way of watching out for him. Strangely, he took some comfort in letting Betty take the reins at times. Edward cocked his head and narrowed his eyes. "All right, Mrs. Curtis, who is paying for this dinner?"

Betty giggled and headed for the car. "You are, and I promise you will love the company. It's not every day you get to be seen with the likes of a woman like me."

Edward laughed heartily. "I can't argue with that."

Riding through the narrow streets, Edward looked out of his window and wondered why he did not miss riding in cars any longer. Betty talked endlessly about matters he cared nothing about. At times he either nodded his agreement or brought forth a slight grunt to make her feel he was still listening. Betty stopped at the Cloth Barn and gathered a few things. She hoped he didn't mind, but there were still a few places she needed to stop and "pick up a few things."

Time passed slowly at first and then gained momentum. Before the last stop was finished, he realized it was nearly time for lunch. Betty opened the car door and placed more bags on the rear seat. Edward wondered if there was anything left in the small town for someone else to buy. With a heavy sigh, she started the engine and headed for Cliff's Diner.

Nobody ever used the actual name, Cliff's Chicken and Beef, for the restaurant except tourist. Edward had known Cliff's father when he first opened the diner in 1958. It was the only restaurant in the vicinity that was open on Sundays. The outcry from the Bible thumpers could be heard across the valley. Cliff's father told the city council to mind their own business. He had every right to feed the people of the community. The war lasted for two weeks, and then the people who cried the loudest were the first customers through the door after church.

Edward and Betty entered the diner and spotted a booth by the window. Without a word or waiting to be seated, she walked over to the booth and sat down. Cliff stood by the register and caught the waitress on her way to the booth. "Let me greet these people, and I'll get back with you." The waitress nodded politely and stepped over to another table.

The smile on Cliff's face was genuine. He had a way of putting his customers at ease and rarely forgot a name. "Mr. Caulfield, how are you today? It's been a while since you have been to see us."

Edward smiled back and reached for the menu in Cliff's hands. "I have been doing very well, thank you. I brought my keeper with me today. She loves your baked chicken. I hate to tell her your dad always used pigeons."

Cliff laughed loudly. "I tried the pigeon, but the chicken was cheaper."

Betty snarled, "Both of you are very funny. Red Skelton you ain't. Now, Cliff, I want your baked chicken with gravy and everything that goes with it. Don't forget my sweet tea."

Cliff grinned. "I will get you the best dish in the house, Mrs. Curtis. You don't have to worry about a thing here."

The waitress wasted no time getting the orders for Edward and Betty. The smile on Betty's plump face was a joy to see. Cliff's restaurant had been remodeled on several occasions. Currently, he was experimenting with a purely mountain theme with a touch of the Native American. He was a man who insisted on keeping up with change. As society changed, so did Cliff. It was a very good reason why tourists came year after year to eat here. Not to mention the food and prices were excellent.

Chapter Five

Betty spent her day cleaning Edward's old home and was well pleased with her accomplishments. There were bird's nests here and there that were cleaned out and disposed of. Buck repaired the windows as promised and made arrangements with Edward to return and repair the back porch by replacing the rotting wood.

Edward beamed with pride when he entered the house. You would never have known it could look so good. Betty sat in the kitchen drinking a cup of coffee. As Edward entered the door, his nose led him straight to the aroma of fresh coffee. Betty poured another cup for herself and a cup for Edward. "Mr. Edward, do you approve of your home today?"

Edward nodded and spoke to her with pride in his voice. "Betty, what would I do without you? The house is magnificent. I thought it would never look the same again, but you proved me wrong."

Betty blushed and swiped her hand at his knee. "You are just tryin' to get on my good side. You take a girl to dinner and then get her to clean your house. You ain't got even a smidgen of shame about you."

Edward snickered. "I think you really like the attention, you just won't admit it."

Betty eased out of her chair and picked up her dustpan. "Okay, you got me, old man, but I'll never admit you were right."

Betty turned slightly in her tracks and lowered her voice. "I put sheets on your bed upstairs. I reckoned you might like to spend the night here tonight for a change. If you want me to stay, I can put another set of sheets on the bed in the guest room across the hall from you."

Edward was amused at the suggestion, but still he felt like it may be a good thing for him. The feelings were mixed, and he wondered if it was the right thing to do. Betty stood silently waiting for his answer. Edward pushed his chair back from the table and then headed for the door. Looking back, he told Betty he would let her know his answer before the end of the day.

Edward returned to his chair beneath the oak by the river. Pulling his hat low across his eyes, he began to doze. The sound of the water rolling over the stones lulled him into a sense of euphoria. He knew there was nowhere on God's green earth he would rather be.

Without hesitation, he jumped from his chair and returned to the house. He found Betty putting sheets on the bed in the guest room. Standing in the doorway, he laughed at the large woman bent over in front of him adjusting the sheets. "Betty, you know me too well. Thank you. We'll go into town and pick up something to eat for in the morning."

Betty fluffed the last pillow and gathered her cleaning materials. "I'm way ahead of you, Mr. Edward. The last stop we made was for here. I figured you need a break from your routine. You go sit yourself down and I'll get supper for you."

Edward nodded and made his way downstairs and out of the back door. He had a spring in his step today. Stopping in mid-stride, he suddenly remembered something he was fond of doing ages ago. Turning on his heel, he went back to the house. Edward passed the staircase and entered the dining room. On the opposite wall the door led into a small room he once used as his office and library.

The freshly oiled trim work fairly shone in the sunlight filtering through the window. To the right of the door was a tiny closet. He rushed over and turned the handle gently. To his surprise, it opened easily at his touch. Reaching deep inside, he pulled a dusty banjo from the corner. He could not seem to remove the smile from his face. It was not unlike greeting a friend from the past. Edward looked around the room until he found a soft cloth that Betty had forgotten when she cleaned his office. Carefully he wiped the dust from the banjo and then exited the house.

Betty was just finishing the upstairs when she heard Edward rambling through the house. She stood wondering what he could be doing. It had been many years since she had seen his spirits rise as they had today. There were times she felt as though he should have never left this house. It didn't matter to her what doctors and friends had to say. Advice was just someone else's opinion. She only wanted what was best for Edward and to do what made him happy. Edward was all she had, and she knew it well.

Stopping in her tracks, she cocked her head trying to hear what she thought was music coming from behind the barn. It was music! She was sure of it. Edward used to play the banjo years ago, but she had not seen him pick up an instrument all the days she had known him. There was no mistaking the sounds of the melodies being played on a banjo. Betty laughed loudly and could not stop. Something had brought him back to life, if only for this short while. The banjo strings danced beneath his fingers, and Betty did a jig to the tune of "Mountain Girls." Still laughing giddily, she realized she felt stirrings she had thought were long gone. She wanted to dance, and imagined herself as a young girl again. Once back downstairs, she danced her way to the kitchen and stood close by the screen door, listening to the music Edward was playing.

Still not believing her ears, she cooked their supper and waited for Edward to return. Betty would not have interrupted his pleasures for anything at this moment in time. Humming to herself, she set the plates on the table and placed Edward's silverware next to his plate. She had forgotten the salt and pepper shakers and turned toward the stovetop to retrieve them. Returning to the table, Betty stopped short in her tracks.

The dinner plate and silverware were moving by unseen hands to the chair by the window. A cold shiver raced down her spine as she searched the room for someone pulling a prank on her. There was no one in the room to cause this to happen. The sound of the rusty spring on the screen door screeching brought her back to reality.

Edward stood staring at her as though she had lost her mind. "Betty, you are white as a sheet. Maybe you are the one who needs the rest instead of me."

Betty found it difficult to speak. When she found her voice, she told him to wash his hands and get ready for supper. Only silence accompanied her actions afterward.

Edward washed his hands at the kitchen sink and sat in his chair. "Betty, how did you know I always sat in this chair at supper?"

Betty's faced turned pale once more, and she lied easily. "You probably don't remember you told me."

Edward grinned as he lifted his fork to get a chicken leg from the platter in front of him. "I do a lot of things these days I can't seem to remember. Either way, it feels good to be eating at my table again. I could have sworn I smelled bread baking when I was coming back from the barn."

"I made biscuits, Mr. Edward. I never did learn how to make good bread dough. I hope you ain't disappointed." His words had cut deep into Betty, who knew his wife always baked fresh bread for him. She was not going to tell him she had not placed his plate at the chair or that she had seen it being placed there by unseen hands.

A cold chill raced down her spine once again. Betty felt as if a tiny hand had patted her cheek in approval of her decision not to speak of what had happened.

Edward finished his meal and gulped the last of the sweet tea. "That was a mighty fine meal, Mrs. Curtis. My compliments to the chef I fear are not nearly sufficient for the pleasures of that meal."

Betty blushed. Her plump cheeks were reddening deeply. "Get out of here so I can get the dishes done and sit for a spell myself."

Edward pushed his chair back gently and pulled his pipe from his pocket. Packing his pipe as he left the kitchen, he walked slowly back through the house and out of the front door. Betty had left one of the cane-backed chairs by the end of the porch. Edward settled himself in it and lighted his pipe. The match flared briefly as he placed it to the bowl. He drew in slowly and gently. The smell of sweetbriar tobacco wafted through the air about him.

The sight that lay before his aging eyes was far from reality. The valley where he had built his home was well-known for an abundance of sweet grass. The unique essence of the plant soothed his senses. The aroma of sweet grass in the air took him far away, down the dusty lanes of time. The vision of his sister walking across the meadow, waving to him as she disappeared behind the garden wall brought his mind ever farther from his position in life. Disregarding what he knew in his soul to be true, he ignored his feelings and ventured to live this dream for a while longer.

Edward's eyes drifted to the old tree by the river and saw his hound lying in the shade, sleeping. He nearly called out to him to come and sit with him. A shuffling from his left brought his vision to alight on the hound now beside of his chair. Edward did not care the hound was no longer in the shade of the tree. He was content just to know his dog was close to him as it should be.

The song of the birds in the trees was just another reason to continue down this road of precious memories. In his mind, all the flowers were in full bloom and nothing could be any prettier than the world before him. Absently, he reached down and patted his hound on his haunches. The warmth of the dog could be felt. In Edward's mind, this was not a dream, and he never wanted to leave his chair and relinquish the things that were his, and his alone.

Betty eased through the front door and stood watching him as he traveled through time. She knew by the look in his eyes that he was looking back at times that were precious for him. Quietly she slipped back into the house and left Edward to his thoughts.

Edward envisioned his former life with Celia. He tried to recall every second of his life here with her. Closing his eyes, he could smell her perfume and feel the warmth of her touch. He thought of her every move. Her laughter rang in his ears. Her face appeared to him clearly in his mind's eye. The ice-blue eyes adorning her face came ever closer to him. Her lips parted slightly and were about to touch his own when he awoke with a start.

Edward realized teardrops had begun to form in his eyes. He wondered how he could have been so foolish as to believe he could bring back so many memories without having an adverse effect on his broken heart. Relighting his pipe, he leaned forward and stared at his withered hands. They were the hands of a man who had labored all of his life, and now the seeds of time had started to grow. It was a feeling of being so far out of touch with all he still felt he needed to do with his life.

Betty called out to Edward to come inside before the rain began. Looking up at the sky, he realized he had been too far away to notice dark clouds had moved in and a gentle breeze was bringing in the rain. Rising from his chair, he wandered back into the house and flopped himself into his favorite chair.

Betty had made a small fire in the fireplace to take away the dampness pervading the room. Edward noticed she had placed his afternoon newspaper on the table by his chair. He could not ask for a better companion in his life. She anticipated his every move and doted on him. In the same breath, she was quick to assure him he was his own man and did not need her.

The time slowly passed with the ticking of the clock in the hallway. Betty quietly rose from her chair and left Edward dozing in his chair. He would go to his bed when he was ready and needed no help from her to make his way up the stairs. She stirred the small fire back to life and placed a few pieces of firewood on the hot embers to keep him warm until it was time for him to go to bed for the night.

The patter of the rain falling outside of his window had lulled Edward into a deep sleep. The burst of energy he had experienced earlier in the day had passed, and his body felt tired and weak. Opening his eyes slowly, he looked about him and found he was still in his chair before a warming fire in the fireplace. Betty had seen fit not to wake him, and he was grateful for that. The small lamp on the table by the far end of the sofa cast shadows on the far wall. For a brief instant he could have sworn he saw a shadow glide across the room and travel behind his chair. He called out softly, "Is that you, Betty?" Only silence greeted him in return.

Dismissing the notion Betty was still rambling around the house, Edward eased back into his chair and watched the flames of the fire dancing within the hearth.

The house echoed the ticking of the clock on the mantel. The silence surrounding him with only the sound of the clock was almost surreal. There was a presence in the room he gradually became aware of. His senses were piqued as he felt a chill in the air about him. A whisper soft as the morning dew touched his ear: "Edward."

Edward refused to move. "Celia, have you come to me again?"

Celia spoke softly spoke to him. "Yes, Edward, I am here."

A gentle smile crossed his face. "I am so glad to hear your voice. Can you stay for a while?"

A heavy sigh was heard in the room about him. "I will stay as long as I can. That is all I can promise."

"Were you here today, my love?" he asked gently.

"Yes, I tried to kiss you once more and was pulled away." She sighed.

"I thought it was a dream." Edward looked about the room, trying to catch a glimpse of her.

"Edward, you cannot see me as I am. Rest yourself, my love, and be grateful for this time." Celia's voice came from everywhere at once.

"Celia, is it really you the others see dancing in the mist?" he asked.

"It is I, Edward, as I have assured you before. I am waiting for you. We will be together again in a far better place than this," she whispered.

Edward stood to his feet. "I couldn't understand what you said, my love. Please tell me again."

The voice came once again from a far distance. "Know that I am here, and be thankful for this short time."

Edward begged with his voice nearly failing him. "Please don't go, Celia." The silence that followed left a mournful moan deep in his throat because he knew she had left him.

With the sorrow of losing her still deep in his heart, he climbed the stairs to his room and lay down for the rest of the night. Sleep evaded him as he wrestled with the reasoning of why he could hear Celia and still not be able to see her.

The next morning started early for Edward. He felt weak from having slept fitfully through the night. Edward stayed close by the house until the rotting boards on the back porch could be repaired. Buck had been able to get to his repairs sooner than expected. Edward was grateful and gave him a few extra dollars for his services.

Betty had neatly packed everything into her car and stood by the front porch admiring the day. A slight breeze was in the air with the aroma of mountain sweet grass. There were times when she prayed she could slow time for just a small while. She knew one day her time here would end, and her heart yearned for a place in heaven as pleasant as these mountains.

Edward cleared his throat as he rounded the corner of the house. Buck followed close behind and tipped his hat as he passed by Betty's side. Betty smiled and waved good-bye.

"I guess that will take care of things for now, Betty," Edward said.

Betty breathed a sigh of relief. "Yesterday almost did me in for sure. The house is bigger than I remembered. If you're ready, we'll get back to the house so I can catch up on my work there."

Edward nodded in agreement and crawled in on the driver's side of the car. Betty said nothing, but her eyes betrayed a small fear. His driving techniques left a lot to be desired these days.

Edward drove slowly down the path, doing his best to avoid as many ruts in the road as possible. Betty watched the scenery as they passed by the river. With little more than a second thought, she blurted out, "Who were you talking to last night, Edward?"

Edward was taken aback for an instant. "I wasn't talking to anybody. Why do you ask?" He did not want to lie to her, and yet he did not feel he was bound to reveal everything to her.

Betty sighed. "Mr. Edward, you were talking to somebody last night after I went to bed. I know you were because I heard two voices, not just yours."

Edward never turned his eyes from the road as he spoke to her. "Betty, you were really tired after all that work yesterday. I expect you fell asleep right away and were dreaming. You and I were the only people in the house, and we didn't have any visitors that late at night."

Betty grinned slyly. "You ain't much of a liar, old man. I know what I heard. I was awake when I heard you talkin'. For your information, I never said what time I heard it."

Edward pursed his lips and remained silent for the rest of the journey home. Betty let the subject drop for the time being. Sooner or later, he would tell her the truth. He always did.

The next two weeks were filled with Edward keeping his appointments about town. He worked in the yard and gave it a wonderful cleaning. He and Betty traveled to a nursery in Murphy and purchased more plants for the cottage. At the end of the day, he felt better about himself. Physically he was bordering on being a total wreck, but his mind was at peace.

Betty had always wanted a house with a white picket fence bordering the yard. Edward made her wish come true. He sent her on some errands for him in Asheville. By the time she returned, Buck Queen had built a magnificent white picket fence with an ornate trellis and a wrought-iron entrance. Betty cried softly as she hugged Edward and thanked him for such a grand surprise.

In the evening, Betty brought a plate of her cookies and a cold glass of milk onto the porch. She placed the plate on the wicker table next to his rocking chair and walked away grinning. *When the old coot wakes up, he'll think I'm tryin' to poison him.* She held back her laughter until she reached the kitchen and was out of his hearing.

Micheal Rivers

Chapter Six

Two weeks had passed, and Lena was eager to see her friend once more. Her cabin was closing in on her quickly. She tried to occupy her time with other things. Traveling through the mountains, she photographed the waterfalls and hiked well-worn trails. The discovery of ancient roads from early settlers and the Indians intrigued her.

Sitting on a huge boulder overlooking the valley below, she tried to envision what the area looked like to the first immigrants here. She knew the Cherokee and the Catawba Indians saw these same sights long before the first settlers ever dreamed of being here. Old tintype photos could have never done any justice to what lay before her eyes. So many changes through the centuries had taken place, and yet all had not been spoiled by man. Lena watched the morning sun rise above the Blue Ridge Mountains from her lofty perch. The multitude of colors cascading through the sky gave birth to a new day in a world filled with the pursuit of contentment.

Checking her watch, Lena climbed from her perch and hiked back to her car. She had made plans to meet Edward after lunch and had no desire to miss her meeting with him. They had much to share with each other, and she felt better for doing so already.

Edward was an enigma. His gentle manner and sense of humor made him a pleasure to talk with. She never felt he was trying to force her to bend to his will. When she had no desire to talk, he was content to just sit and watch the grass grow. Her life had been filled with people who had not the slightest idea when to shut up and listen. They heard but they never listened.

Within an hour, Lena arrived at the end of the path leading to Edward's former home. The old house loomed before her as she searched the yard for Edward. Not seeing him, she felt she may have arrived ahead of him.

Then Edward's voice came to her from the front porch. "Good to see you, Lena. I was hoping you received my message. When you weren't here, I thought you may have gone home for a bit."

Lena turned to see Edward coming out of the front door of the house, closing it behind him as he stepped farther onto the porch. "No, I was just running a little late."

Brushing her hair back from her eyes with back of her hand, she smiled sweetly. "I see you have been doing some cleaning here. I hope you didn't do it on my account."

Edward shook his head and pushed his hat higher up on his forehead. "No, it's just that time of year for me. I try to keep up as much as possible. I'm glad to see you are wearing your hiking shoes. I have something to show you today."

Lena was puzzled as to what it could be. Looking down at her hiking boots, she chuckled. "I don't know about fashion, but these aren't worth a darn for dancing."

"The boots are perfect for today. Shall we go?"

Lena grinned broadly. "By all means."

Edward joined her midway in the front yard and turned her toward the ridge. They walked in silence through the woods surrounding them. A well-worn path greeted her at every turn. Her curiosity was piqued when they came to a small clearing and turned back toward the river. Ahead of her, she heard the sound of rushing water. Just as they both cleared the tree line, Lena saw a narrow wooden bridge crossing the river. It had the look of being centuries old, but the handrails were surprisingly solid to the touch. The bridge itself had seen a few repairs, but nothing major. Lena felt as though she had stepped into another world.

"This is what I wanted you to see. This, and what lies up the trail to your left. This is a special place. Always has been for many," Edward said.

Lena stood in awe. "I can't believe this. Is this your land also?"

Edward snorted. "Of course, I don't believe in trespassing." He laughed aloud at her amazement. "Around that bend is a place called Angel Falls. We'll visit it another day. There is a legend here that very few know. As I said, this is a special place. The Indians came here long ago to find their path in life. If the legend is true, you come to this place on a lovers' moon and pray. After your prayers have been said, you give your heart to the spirits here to tell your lot in life. You will then fall asleep, and your future is told to you. If the prophecy is truth, then you will hear the spirits sing from the waters of the falls."

Lena stood listening to his every word. "Did you ever hear the spirits sing?"

Edward stared down at his feet and tried to keep from answering her. His efforts were in vain. She prodded him gently until he answered her.

"Yes, I heard the spirits sing when I was a young man. You have to understand, Lena. You may not get the future you desire from the spirits here. In my opinion, it is better not to know. I can say the spirits do not lie."

Lena stared at the rolling waters beneath the bridge. Edward interrupted her thoughts. "I know what you are thinking. It may not be wise to follow through. I still feel it is better not to know."

After a short time on the bridge, the two of them returned to the house and gathered some much-needed rest beneath the tree.

"Okay, Edward, when do I get the grand tour of the Caulfield estate?"

"There is not much of an estate here, young lady. The palace lies yonder by the glen. Sorry, the moat no longer has legendary lizards to charm you. You will find trout in the stream and biscuits on the table. Coupons are available at the door for any and all local restaurants and spas. You must be accompanied by an adult, and the castle closes at six." Edward chuckled at his own joke.

Lena leaned forward. "That was quite a spiel for a youngster your age. Do you have valet parking?"

Edward turned serious. "Madam, you have to be kidding me. We not only have valet parking but the valet gets to keep the car."

Lena laughed gently and touched his arm. "You did not answer my question, kind sir. So I will have to be blunt or have my attorney contact you. Do I get to see the house?"

Edward turned and grimaced. "Of course you do, all you had to do was ask."

The paint on the outside of the house had faded badly and did not honor what the interior of the house had to offer. Entering the front door, Lena stepped into the foyer. She had been expecting an average country home. Her first impression of the staircase in front of her was the look and feel of a man with very distinguished taste. The rich color of cherry-wood trim work was everywhere. Lena lightly fingered the stucco walls and glanced around her. It was truly beautiful. The craftsmanship was unequaled in her eyes.

Edward beamed with pride. "At the end of the foyer, you see the two double doors. When these are open, they allow your guests directly into the formal dining room without having to venture through other rooms first."

Giving Lena time to examine the paintings on the wall, Edward continued. "The paintings you see here are Dutch. I purchased two of them on a trip to Holland some years back. The gentleman in the portrait is my great grandfather."

Lena wanted badly to admire the table in the center of the foyer more closely. Edward was well aware where her attention lay. "I built this table for Celia the first year we were married. She loved to keep fresh flowers here in a vase that belonged to her mother."

Edward drew her attention to their right. "This is the living room. I tried to set the house in such a manner that a pleasant sight was to be seen from anywhere in the house. Celia preferred to have her chair by the fireplace. That is the reason for this chair being here."

Lena admired the delicate trim throughout the room. "Where were you able to find wood trim as beautiful as this? It appears to be hand-carved."

Edward smiled proudly. "All of the wood trim throughout the house *is* hand-carved. I carved each and every piece of it myself. The stonework on the fireplace was produced by a master mason from Nantahala. It was one of the last fireplaces he ever built before he died. The mantel was given to me as a wedding present from my father."

Lena could not help inquiring about the flooring of the rooms. "I understand you no longer live here full-time, Edward.

Forgive me for asking, but how do you keep these floors looking like new?"

"That is attributed to my best friend and companion, Betty. Without her, I would never be able to keep the house alive. The wood of these floors helps also. I had every one of them planed and sized perfectly at the mill for Celia. I wanted everything to be perfect for her. The flooring is two inches thick and is solid oak. There are no nails in the entire house. Everything is pegged as it was in the older days of my ancestors.

"I built this house when I was twenty years old. It was the same year Celia and I married. Three men from my father's mill helped me with the process and assured me it would be ready for her before the marriage was ever consummated.

"There have been a few updates over the years, but they were all minor. The kitchen, naturally, has been updated, as well as the toilets. I did replace the chandelier in the dining room due to rust that could not be removed without damaging the piece. Everything you see in the house is original, right down to the furniture."

The colors in the room blended well. Celia was a woman who knew what was pleasing to the eye. No doubt the curtains, though expensive for the time, needed replacing badly. To Edward's eyes, everything was still as it was when Celia graced these rooms with her presence.

Lena was wise in keeping these opinions to herself. She did not want to hurt Edward in any way. She followed Edward through the house slowly. The next room was small but very comfortable. There were delicate figurines on a corner shelf and a chair with a bolt of green cloth on the floor directly beneath it. The window looked out on the flower garden in the side yard. She had not seen this garden before. It was placed in such a manner as to be seen only from this window. Across from the chair that was placed so the view of the garden was unobstructed was a small wing-backed Victorian chair. A rich brocade adorned the wood, and you could almost envision Celia sitting there sewing during the day. Her sewing basket still lay beside the chair, waiting for her.

Edward cleared his throat. "As you can see, this was Celia's sewing room. She made all of her own dresses, and I would dare to compare them to anything a seamstress could ever produce today. You will see some of the dresses when we go upstairs.

"You are the first woman, other than Betty, here since she left me. I hope she approves. The room beyond this is the kitchen, with a separate entry leading to the dining room for serving."

Entering the kitchen, Lena felt a twinge of nostalgia. A step back in time that was pleasing to her senses. Above the sink was a plaque with Celia's name carved into it. On each side of her name were hand-carved Celtic crosses and flowers in full bloom. The kitchen window over the sink introduced a view of the valley behind the house and the mountains in the distance. The cabinets gleamed in the kitchen light. She was not sure, but they appeared to be made of African rosewood.

Edward stood by quietly and watched her as she breathed in the essence of Celia's kitchen. Then he spread his hands in a gesture to cover everything in the room. "This was a point of pride for Celia. It was one of the first things she showed her mother."

Lena nodded her approval. "I can certainly understand why. It is a paradise for a woman who loves to cook."

Edward grunted his approval and opened the door to the formal dining room. "The dining-room table was built by my grandfather. If you will notice the legs of the table, you will see a machine never touched the wood. He carved every piece himself, and the stain for the table was a formula he developed himself. Nothing that I am aware of can match this. His work was well-known in England, and there are few pieces of it left for the world to see. I was able to find out that a museum in London has a dressing table he built. For what reason, I do not know. I never got around to finding the reason.

"The portrait on the wall behind you is my grandfather. I felt he deserved a place of honor next to his work. The lady next to him is his wife. Their names were Ambrosia and Victoria Caulfield. He was the builder of all the furniture in this room except for one of the dining chairs. It was broken badly, and I tried to duplicate his work and replace it. I found out very quickly I was not the master he was by any means."

Lena looked the chair over carefully. "I cannot find a flaw in this chair, Edward."

Edward's eyebrows furrowed slightly. "I know each and every flaw. Believe me when I tell you the chair would never stand up to the quality of his craftsmanship."

Lena followed Edward through another set of double doors leading from the dining room and into a cozy room designed strictly for men. It was a smoking room. The aroma of pipe tobacco was still in the air. The room was paneled in rich-colored wood that accented a world where matters of importance may have been discussed. The leather chairs were placed in such a manner that it was obvious men came here to talk and be themselves. A small library of books covered the entire wall opposite the doorway. Many were leather-bound editions of great value. Lena noticed this was the only room she had seen with a rug on the floor. It was a genuine Persian carpet in mint condition.

Edward smiled. "This is the room where I came to relax and sometimes study the woes of the world. The Persian carpet was a gift to me from my youngest sister. I have to admit, she was always my favorite. I called her my pearl because of the color of her skin. She designed this room and bought almost everything you see here.

"Many of the books are mine. The leather-bound volumes you see were presents from her. She always said I was to read them and remember her when she was not around. She would be surprised at the amount of time I have spent thinking of her."

"Has she been gone long?" Lena asked gently.

Edward thought for a moment. "I would say she has been gone longer than I care to remember. She came to stay with me one summer and try to keep me company. I must say it was pleasant to have her around the house. I knew she would be going home at the end of summer. I was wrong about that.

"The garden wall you saw at the end of the yard has a stone walkway on the other side so you can walk there without getting your shoes wet after the rain. It is a very pleasant walk on a sunny day, and she spent a lot of time there. I built a swing for her to rest on when she was there. I was sitting on the porch smoking my pipe on a Sunday morning when she came out of the house. She said she was going to the garden and asked me to walk with her for a while. I was very tired and just wanted to stay where I was, so I begged off. She laughed happily and strolled across the yard. Just before she reached the wall, she turned to me with a big smile on her face and waved. I waved back to her and watched her go around the corner of the wall. It was the last time I ever talked to her."

"What happened?" Lena asked.

"I never knew this would be her last visit anywhere. She knew she was going to die, but not when. The doctors told her she had cancer and there was nothing they could do for her. She decided to spend some time here with me instead of being alone in a hospital somewhere. She died much sooner than the doctors expected. I found her sitting in the swing. I thought she was sleeping. You remind me of her in so many ways."

Lena spoke gently. "Thank you, Edward. I appreciate the compliment."

Edward picked up a small picture on the table next to one of the chairs. "This is a photograph of her when she was much younger and in good health."

Lena held the picture in her hands and looked deeply into the woman's face. Edward was correct in his observations; she looked very much like herself. Handing the picture back to Edward, Lena started for the next door. "Where does this door lead?"

Edward stepped forward and opened the door for her. "This is my office. Not much to see, but I spent a lot of time here. I always tried to stay ahead of the game."

Lena suddenly giggled aloud. She had spied his banjo standing in the corner of the room. "Ah, a man of music. Can you play this, or is it just for show?"

Edward blushed. "Yes, I used to play it often, but I didn't pick it up again until a couple of weeks ago."

Lena grabbed his arm and pulled him close to her. "Okay, so now you are obliged to play for me sometime."

"I will give it some consideration. Shall we move on?" Edward said flatly.

There were a lot of pictures of faces Edward did not introduce her to. She knew eventually he would explain who they were and their connections to him. The next room opened into a well-lit formal sitting room. The natural light filled the room, accenting everything about it.

"Celia told me a woman must have a place to entertain the ladies as well as family. This room is hers alone. She enjoyed this room almost more than any other, in my opinion. I loved looking at her face when she was fussing with the furniture and the little figurines and such when she was in here. The pillows on the sofa had to be just right, and I could not sit on the furniture in anything but my Sunday clothes, as she called them."

Lena would love to have known Celia. With all she had seen and heard, she knew in her heart Celia was no ordinary lady.

Edward waved his hand in the air. "This is about all for the downstairs; there are four rooms upstairs and a porch you can walk out on and enjoy the view. The master bedroom is very large with an area where you can sit by the fireplace when the nights are cold and you want to read a good book." This being said, Edward walked with her up the stairs and into the main hallway.

Looking down the hallway, Lena could see another set of glassed double doors. Edward pointed to the doors and spoke to her quietly. "Those doors at the end lead to another small porch over Celia's garden. This door on your right is the master bedroom."

Edward made no move to show her the master bedroom, and she did not wish to try to force the issue. There were some places that should be respected. This was another segment of his private life and should be kept as such.

The other bedrooms were not lavish, but they were far from ordinary. The décor was antiquated yet still showed good taste, the very same as with the rest of the home's paintings and photographs adorning the walls. Another short hallway was built between two of the bedrooms. This hallway led to the porch over the front door. From this location, the river was seen clearly rolling by the front of the house. Very pleasant indeed for any and all who came here to sit and relax.

Returning back down the hallway, Lena asked about using the toilet. Edward laughed. "It is the next door up on the left."

Lena traveled the hallway and grabbed the door handle, turning it quickly. A voice behind her stopped her hand.

"This is not the door. It is the next one. This door leads to the widow's walk."

Lena apologized and moved forward.

Edward waited in the hallway for her return. He wondered how much time he had lost by not paying attention to any of the little things. This young lady had noticed things about Celia he had not seen for himself.

Returning refreshed, Lena asked if she could see the widow's walk. Edward was quick to tell her this was one of the points of the house he wanted her to see more than others. Beyond the door was a wide winding staircase. Climbing the few steps to the landing, Edward pulled a key from his pocket and unlocked the door. The door swung open easily and allowed them to enter. This room was far different than any of the others in the house. The small room was surrounded with glass panels on three sides, and there was a door leading to the widow's walk.

The room was furnished with two chairs and a love seat. Two small tables, one between the chairs and the other by the door, were set with candles placed in pewter candleholders. The fireplace was small but more than adequate for the room. Above the mantel was a portrait of a very lovely woman dressed in a white high-collared dress. The intricate lace on the dress was perfectly done. Her hair was placed high on her head with a necklace of gold and sapphires against her skin. This painting held the quality of no ordinary artist.

Edward placed his hand on the mantel and turned to face Lena. "I would like to introduce to you my wife, Celia."

The look in his eyes told Lena that Edward still adored the woman in the painting more than anyone could ever possibly imagine. It broke her heart to see him yearning for her as he did. At this moment she would have traded the world just for Edward to be able to have Celia back with him.

Edward glanced toward the door and pointed. "We will go this way, and you will have the surprise of your life."

Lena stepped to the door and stood, spellbound. Edward spoke as if words were never enough for what Lena was witnessing. "What you are seeing right now is where you were earlier today. That is Angel Falls in front of you. From this height there are many sights to be seen. However, this walk was built so Celia could visit the falls at any time she desired."

It was truly a vision that would never be duplicated in any form. Lena understood perfectly why the both of them would come here. If there was truly a place in heaven for them, it would certainly look like this. "Edward, how did you meet Celia?"

Edward ignored the question and escorted her back through the glass door. "I am feeling a little tired now. We'll continue this on another day, if you don't mind."

Lena agreed it had been a long day, and she too was tired. They agreed to meet again on the following Monday.

Micheal Rivers

Chapter Seven

The weekend was spent lounging in his favorite chair while Betty engrossed herself in movies. She drew pleasure from watching the old stars perform on the screen. Lana Turner was her idol at one time, and Betty felt she was the most beautiful woman in the world. These days, instead of Ray Milan, she would gladly watch Brad Pitt over any of the male stars. Edward would tease her with no mercy. "Betty, I'm inviting Brad over for supper. Can you make your pot roast again?"

Betty would then find something to throw at him and run him out onto the porch. Edward would laugh at her reactions until his sides ached.

Edward sat and rocked in his chair, watching cars cruise slowly down his street. It was a pleasant weekend to just sit and rock. The blue of the Carolina sky reminded him so much of Celia's eyes. Her eyes bordered on being ice blue, and the sky above him today was just that.

He thought back on the times he and Celia would go for a drive on days such as this. They loved to make a picnic lunch and stop on a nearby mountaintop they were fond of. It was a world where the only people who existed were Celia and Edward. He held her hand and they spoke of their love for each other. They assured themselves the future was going to be the best anyone could ever ask for.

Edward hung his head and wondered why she had been taken from him so soon. He understood the Lord worked in mysterious ways, but still he felt cheated. He wanted to give her everything and keep her safe from the world. He could not keep his promise to her, and that hurt more than anything he could possibly imagine. The thought of losing her turned his heart cold. It was a hard life being alone, and he knew nobody would ever fill that void except Celia. His heart belonged to her, and always would until he was called to meet his maker.

Betty called out from the living room and asked him to come inside. Raising himself slowly from the chair, he opened the screen door and passed into the cool breeze coming through the living-room window. Betty said there was a phone call from

Lena for him. Reaching out to him, Betty let him know the young girl sounded upset.

Edward picked up the receiver and listened carefully to Lena on the other end of the line. He said little and hung up slowly at the end of the conversation. Edward looked worried, and Betty inquired if he was feeling ill. Edward told her he was feeling fine, but he was very angry. Without having to be prompted, he told Betty everything Lena had said.

"Lena had returned home for the weekend to surprise her husband and talk for a while. When she arrived, he was not home and a suitcase he used for traveling was missing along with his best clothing. Lena thought in the beginning he had been called away on business. Her husband came home around midnight and had no idea she was there. She walked into the hallway as her husband and his date walked through the door. His date was his secretary, and she was wearing Lena's best evening dress and her jewelry.

"Needless to say, things became very ugly and the police were called. The secretary wants to press charges against Lena for threatening her. The pitiful part of the whole deal is the husband is agreeing with the secretary."

Betty sat, dumbfounded. "Are you sure you heard all that right, Mr. Edward?"

Edward nodded. "Yes, I did. I asked if she needed any help and offered to come and get her. She said she would be all right and will talk to me some more on Monday."

Betty's face reddened with anger. "Did that so-and-so hurt that little girl?"

Edward shook his head. "No, he didn't hit her or anything like that, but from what she said I would not doubt he possibly would. I may be wrong, I don't know."

For the remainder of the day and into the evening, Betty and Edward discussed what could be happening to Lena. Edward remarked about her father. He felt any man worth his salt would go and kick his son-in-law's butt all over the state. It was agreed Edward should not interfere, and still he felt a need to do something for the disrespect Lena had been shown in her own home. Marriage was a sacred vow in Edward's eyes, and no man should be allowed to make a mockery of what God had brought together. Where was it ever written that a man could disrespect his wife and never be berated for his actions? Monday felt as though it would be a long time in coming. For the remainder of the weekend, Edward and Betty thought of nothing but Lena's safety.

Early Monday morning Betty drove Edward to the house by the river. A gentle rain was falling, and she did not want him walking in the rain. Edward had scoffed at the idea of driving there, but Betty won the argument rather easily. Betty told him to use the house today so the two of them would stay dry.

Edward's mind was weary from worrying about her. Betty patted him on the arm and assured him she would be there. "Besides, if she doesn't come, I had the phone turned on so you can call. I'll be there quick as I can," Betty said with a grin.

Edward just shook his head in wonderment. "I never know what you are going to do, so I gave up trying to guess any longer."

Betty laughed happily and shooed him out of the car. She dared not to leave until she saw him safely on the porch.

As she pulled out of the driveway, she spotted a strange car coming up the narrow path. She had no doubt it had to be Lena coming for her visit.

Lena held a haggard look about her. Edward didn't recognize the woman standing before him today. She did not stand erect and look the world in the eye as she was known to do. Lena appeared to him to be a beaten soul, with little or no direction in her life. Edward sat her down in the chair once belonging to Celia and built a small fire to take away the dampness of the room. Betty had placed a thermos of fresh coffee in his basket for them to enjoy. "Are you feeling okay today?" Edward asked gently.

Lena sat trying hard not to cry. She only nodded and stared into the fire. It was an uncomfortable silence that literally filled the room about them. Edward knew she would speak when she was ready and not before.

Nearly an hour had passed before Lena leaned forward slowly and placed her coffee cup on the table beside her. She looked deep into Edward's eyes and spoke quietly. "Will you tell me the story of how you met Celia?"

Edward pushed himself deeper into his chair and lighted his pipe. Lena watched as a ghostly curl of smoke rose from the bowl in his hand.

"I was almost nineteen when I first saw Celia. She had traveled to Robbinsville with her parents to trade a horse they owned. It was a fine horse, but a little nervous around other animals. Her father wanted to trade it for a horse Celia would be able to ride. My oldest brother and I were at the same auction looking for a man who owed my father a great deal of money. We were told to convince him to go and talk to my father before the sheriff was called concerning the debt.

"The day was like any other for the middle of June—the sun baked your brain and turned it into mush in a very short time. I crawled on top of a cattle fence to get a better look around, trying to find the man we were looking for. Just as I found myself sitting steady, I looked toward the stables and saw Celia. She was wearing a yellow sundress and a bonnet to match. When she turned, I saw her face and lost my balance on the fence. Needless to say, my landing was not perfect and my pride was hurt more than anything else. The one thing making matters worse was Celia was a witness to it all. She did not try to conceal her laughter in the slightest. She was the prettiest girl I had ever seen. When I got back to my feet, she had disappeared and I didn't see her again for about two months after.

"One of the wranglers at the stables told me who she was and where she lived. I was shy and not about to go to her house and introduce myself. So, I had to bide my time and hope to see her again. My thoughts were taken throughout my days of her face beneath her sunbonnet.

"I didn't usually go to church on Sunday, but I found the need to start going. I began going to the same church she attended so I could see her. It was a long time before I could work up the courage to talk to her. After a few months, her mother and father gave me permission to come to their home and visit with Celia, and soon the courtship began.

"I asked Celia if she would marry me close to the spot where you sit by the river. I had saved enough money to buy her a small ruby ring and placed it on her finger. She told me I had to ask her parents' permission before we could marry. To her surprise, I had already spoken with them and I was welcomed to the family.

"Three days after she promised she would marry me, I bought this land from one of my father's customers. I knew one day I would build a home for Celia here. Not very long after I asked Celia to marry me, my father passed away. He knew I wanted to marry her and gave me his blessing. He made the mantel for the fireplace as a wedding gift for me before he died. I was barely twenty years old, and 1932 was a hard time for everyone. My father left the mill to me and a little money. The rest of his holdings were spread among the children in our family. I found out much later there was a large sum of money involved.

"I gathered some of the men I trusted, and we built this house for Celia. She was never told about the house until we were almost finished building it. I questioned her several times about what kind of house she dreamed of. Naturally, it sounded much grander than anything I could ever build. I came as close to her dreams as possible. It was a blessing when she said it was more than she could ever have hoped for.

"We didn't have a lot at first. I couldn't afford to buy her the furniture I thought she wanted, so I built most of the things you saw in the house, and friends of mine built other things. We did fair better than most during the Depression. I was very close to losing the mill at one point, and we managed to pull out of the slump. We grew our gardens and sold the extra to help ends meet. I was very lucky to have won a government contract for lumber. This not only kept some of the people here in the community working and feeding their families, but also enabled Celia and I to try to hold on to our dream. Hell, I sound like a rambling old man today."

Lena giggled. "That was far from rambling, and I feel like you are a man who had a reputation he didn't want to lose."

Edward just shrugged his shoulders and looked at her. "What about you, how did you meet your husband?"

Lena shuddered as if she was cold. "The beginning of a nightmare, I must say. His name is Gerald Leicester. My father invited him for dinner on Sundays. You might call it a blind dinner date with chaperones. He was one of the men who worked for my father in one of his companies. He was the kind of man who knew whom to get close to. From what I have seen, he is very good at this.

"These dinners continued until I agreed to go out with him. His charm was more than adequate and he was a very nice-looking man. The push was on with mother, and for whatever reason, father had made his choice for me. I never knew until after we married exactly what he was. It did not take me very long to find out.

"The day we married was the day my mother and father breathed a sigh of relief. They were afraid I would marry someone human. Well, I kissed a frog, and he is still a frog. There was no prince to be found. Time was on his side, and father promoted him almost instantly. He received almost anything he wanted. Gerald has two faces. One face he uses to charm companies out of their money. The other face is nothing but pure greed and evil.

"If it was not for my father, he would be living on the street or in jail for being a con man. A perfect politician if I ever saw one. I know when he lies because his lips are moving. He is the son my father never had, and my mother no longer has to be embarrassed by my actions.

"The wedding reception will forever stand in history as a farce in Richmond society. Gerald saw fit to spend his time with the rich and shameless instead of his new bride. You can imagine the stir it caused among the gossips in the city.

"I could see my future for what is was. Months passed and I told Gerald I wanted a child of my own. I should have shot him first—the reaction would have been the same. He told me he did not want to corrupt a beautiful body with childbearing. He wanted me to stay as I was so I would be perfect when we entertained our guests. It was soon after this conversation he started working more than usual."

Edward shook his head sadly. "Celia and I had a wedding nobody around here will ever forget. It was held in the clearing by the falls. I invited everybody in town to come and see us get married. I think most of them came. We had a grand time of it with dancing and celebrating our marriage. You would have had a lot of fun, I am sure.

"At the end of the evening, Celia and I came back here to sleep in our new home." Edward laughed gently. "We didn't have any money for a honeymoon, but we had each other and a fine new house."

Lena snorted loudly. "Our honeymoon lasted for three weeks in France. I hated the food, I was homesick, and my husband had more eyes for the French girls than he had for me. On the cruise back to the States, he would disappear for hours and curse at me for not being where I could be found easily.

"He managed to win a contract with a large corporation in Idaho while we were on the cruise. Funny thing happened. We had dinner with the CEO and his wife the evening before we returned to port. They did have a very lovely daughter who seemed to take a great deal of interest in Gerald and his charm. Her mother and father didn't seem to notice."

Edward stood from his chair and placed a few more pieces of wood on the fire, bringing it back to life. The gentle warmth of the fire was very comforting. Lena slid back into silence and watched the fire dancing in the hearth. Edward watched her and saw the sadness in her eyes. It seemed as though it reached deep into her soul.

A man must have values to be respected. This Gerald had no morals that Edward could find. Edward was raised to have respect for all until it was proven they could not be respected. He had seen many men in his life, and the roughest of the bunch still protected their families. The man and wife may fuss and fight, but the children were always protected in his world. Lena's father should have looked more closely at Gerald before he gave her hand to him for marriage. With this in mind,

Edward laid his head back on the cushion of the chair and went to sleep.

Edward awoke with a start, hearing the sound of a car horn echoing through the house. Lena was no longer in the chair, and she had left him a note saying she was going home and would return the next day. Edward raised himself slowly from his chair and shuffled to the fireplace. The ashes had grown cold, and he knew the house would be safe. Walking to the door, he opened it slowly and headed out onto the porch.

Chapter Eight

Edward slept fitfully through the night. His dreams turned to feelings of anxiety. It was not a nightmare keeping him from sleeping peacefully but the memories and questions cluttering his thoughts. It was a mad jumble of pictures and words racing through his mind. The mind and the body were unable to find a solace in the arms of Morpheus.

Sitting up, he sat on the side of the bed and lighted his pipe. At times he was able to gain control of his thoughts when he had his pipe. A small wisp of blue smoke curled and danced in the air. The faint light of the moon came across the windowsill like a dream. It was comforting to know this would always be here for him at times such as this. Staring out of the window, he cleared his mind of all things as he studied the stars above.

The night passed quickly, and soon the morning sun was starting up over the tops of the mountains. Edward reached for his clothing, dressing himself hurriedly. A gentle smile crossed his face at the thought of being in the kitchen before Betty. He laughed heartily for he knew this would irritate her to no end. Bouncing out of the door, he slid quietly through the house, avoiding making a single sound for fear of waking her. When he breached the swinging door of the kitchen, his smile slid from his face. Betty was already dressed and making dough for the biscuits.

Without turning, she spoke softly. "I heard you up most of the night. I thought you would be in here early. Figured I would have you a bite to eat time you got here."

Edward grimaced. "There ain't no getting by you, is it?"

Betty giggled. "Nope, and there won't be a day when I don't know what you are up to. You might as well get used to it."

"I thought about heading out a little early today," he said.

"Time you get ready to go, I'll have your lunch basket packed up for you and the little girl." Betty walked over to the stove and threw the cast-iron skillet on top.

Betty and Edward talked of better days and old times as she cooked their breakfast. Edward looked at her sidelong and wondered what was on her mind. After a few minutes of sparring, she finally decided to say what was on her mind. "I got a call from my daughter yesterday. She told me she and her husband had a fallin' out and she was leaving him. Seems he found hisself a little chickie on the side to ease his tensions.

"I had to do something I figured I wouldn't ever be able to do. She asked me if her and the young'uns could come stay here. I told her no, they couldn't. First place, there ain't the room for it, and second place, it ain't my house.

"That won't good enough for her, and she wanted to stay here and you and I stay at the old house. She would pay rent, of course. I still said no, and I got madder than I ever been in my life. I told her she never talked to me 'less she was in trouble, and now here she was. I told her I was too old for such mess, and her and that thing she married needed to get theirselves straightened out like all grown folks do. She done a little beggin', and I felt sorry for her till she asked me for money, then I hung up on her."

Edward could see she was still angry. Now would have been the perfect time for him to set her off for the day, but he could not find it within himself to upset her more than she already was. It was a serious matter for Betty and needed to be handled carefully. "They are adults, Betty. You are correct, they should act as such. I never did care for those on the adulterous side of life. If you need anything, I am here for you, and you know that. I really do not want their troubles in this house. Do you agree?"

Betty nodded slowly. "Yes, I do. I tried my best to get her in the church years ago. If she would have listened to the Lord instead of that friend of hers, she wouldn't be in this fix now. I love my children, but I ain't gonna let them or nobody else walk on me."

Edward grinned and patted her hand. "You are a strong woman, Betty. Did you get the chance to make those cookies yesterday?"

Betty whipped her hand from under his. "Yeah, I did, and you cain't have but two just like Doc Early said."

Edward stood from his chair and walked slowly to the door. "I will be at the coffee shop for a little bit. After that, I will head over to the old house to meet Lena for the rest of the day."

"Would you like for me to drive you up there?" she asked.

"Not today, I feel like walking for a while. I'll let you know when I get back." Edward turned and made his way through the door and onto the porch.

Edward walked slowly down the street of his neighborhood, glancing now and again at the houses lining the streets. Some of these trees had been here before he was ever born. They comforted him like old friends. It was pleasant to walk beneath the shade and remember when things were so very different. It was a time before cars lined the streets, and a young man could hear the sound of horses' hooves as they traveled down the street. The milkman came to your door and delivered fresh milk for you and your family in glass bottles. Ice cream was real and tasted like heaven on hot days. Things had changed so very much, and he longed for even a touch of the days gone by.

The tip of his cane striking a loose stone on the sidewalk brought him back from his thoughts. This was a sad time and a good time for him all rolled into one. He could not understand why he was so dissatisfied with his life at this point in time.

Within minutes, Edward found himself standing just inside the door of the coffee shop and looking for any friends who may have ventured in also. Freddy Wilkes sat in a booth alone by a side window overlooking the street. Edward walked over and sat down across from him. They didn't acknowledge each other's presence until Edward began to drink his coffee.

Freddy blinked at Edward through his thick glasses. "Heard Buck worked on your house the other day."

Edward nodded. "Yes, I had a few windows broken and some wood rot that needed to be fixed."

"You ain't gonna live in it; why don't you sell it?" Freddy snarled.

Edward laughed gently. "Freddy, are you ever in a good mood? If you smile a little, I promise your face won't crack."

Freddy grunted like a hog dining at his trough. "I don't have a lot to smile about, Edward. I'm old, I get in everybody's way, and I can't get it up anymore. I'm like a dog with no teeth on a short chain."

"We all miss what we had before, Freddy. You are certainly not alone. I sat on my front porch the other day and forgot where I was at. Memory is just another item missing from my shelves. You and I both knew we were going to be like this one day. We sat and watched everybody we knew go through the same thing. Doesn't make it easier, but it is something we have to deal with."

Freddy leaned back in the booth and squinted through his glasses, trying to see Edward's face more clearly. "Edward, you didn't change as much as the rest of us. I rarely get to see anybody anymore. I mean that literally. I'm almost blind, and it scares the hell out of me. You and I grew up here and knew everybody. Now, there are so many strangers I can't tell who is who. I built a lot of houses around here when we were young and full of shit. The houses I built are few and far between now. They don't use decent lumber, and you can see through the walls. You walk into a bathroom and everybody in the living room knows when you are taking a crap. That just isn't right.

"This cup of coffee costs me fifty cents. The hell of it is the refill will be another fifty cents. I don't know where we went wrong, but along the line somebody got greedy, and now people like us can hardly make it in this world. Before I got old, I knew when a politician was full of it. Then I tried to trust them. That didn't work either. Now we have people in the White House that just want to play golf and go fishing. To cap all of this off, my butt is forced to be resting in the arms of Medicare."

Edward agreed. "There are too many things in this world that are not right. We did the best we could when we were young, Freddy. We are yesterday's news. We had a couple of presidents to throw the bums out and get us back on track. In these times, everybody is yelling 'pity me,' and the lowlifes live off the taxpayer.

"I don't recall having so many giveaway programs when we were coming along. Either way, it's there and we don't have anything we can do about it."

Freddy signaled to the waitress for another refill. She smiled sweetly as she filled his cup. Edward watched the gleam in Freddy's eye, knowing what he was thinking.

Edward stood and stretched his legs. Making his excuses, he left Freddy sitting in the booth and drooling over the waitress. In his younger days, Freddy was quite the lady's man. To see him now, it could almost break your heart.

Betty stood waiting on the porch with the picnic basket on her lap. Her straw hat leaned to one side in a manner that she had never changed for as long as he had known her. "Going somewhere?" he asked with a grin.

Betty rose from her seat and started down the steps. "I thought I would get you over to the house. You can call me when you get ready to come home."

Without a word, Edward made his way to the car and crawled into the passenger's seat. Edward had tried for years to convince her she needed a new car. Betty was adamant about not getting a newer model. She was used to driving this one and was afraid she would not know how to use another car. Her car was simple, and the newer models did not satisfy her needs. She liked simplicity. In her mind, another minor repair here and there did not warrant a new car.

Reaching the house, Betty pulled into the drive and applied the brakes gently. Edward sat looking at the house for a long moment before reaching for the door handle.

"Is something wrong, Mr. Edward?"

Edward shook his head. "No, Betty, I was just thinking to myself about change. Regardless of what some people think, not everything changes."

Betty had not the slightest idea of what he was referring to, but she decided not to inquire any further.

It was not long after Betty had departed when Edward saw Lena coming down the path to the house. She smiled and waved good-naturedly. She appeared rested and full of energy. It still amazed Edward how much Lena reminded him of his little sister.

Lena shouted out from the yard: "It is a gorgeous day today, Edward."

Edward waved his cane at her, and replied, "Every day is a good day, young lady. You would do well to remember that." He chuckled to himself.

"Today is a big day for you, sir. You get to tell me all about your life with Celia. Are you ready for that?"

Edward sat down on the cane-backed chair Betty had left for him on the porch. "I believe I am. You must promise to not be so bored that you fall asleep again while I am talking."

She looked at Edward with mild surprise. "I would never do that to you, kind sir. But if you fall asleep while you are talking, I am sure to awaken you with a cold glass of water."

"That sounds like a deal if I ever heard one. You must remember, I prefer my ice water with a slice of lime!" Edward laughed aloud at his own joke.

The two of them chatted for a time while enjoying the breeze making its way across the porch. In the distance, birds sang their songs in the trees about them. These sounds intermingled with the waters of the river and created a world of their own.

"Edward, I really want to hear about you and Celia." Lena spoke low, almost in a whisper.

Edward looked off toward the mountaintops and then down to his feet. His scarred hands rested on his knees. It was easy to see he had to prepare what he wanted to say. When it came down to speaking about Celia, he was always reaching deep within himself for the feelings only he could understand and still feel with every breath.

"Celia was and always will be something special in my life. For me, there was no world outside. She was my world in every respect. This is something you must know before you can understand how and why I have lived my life this way.

"When Celia and I married, it was more than a marriage. We had a bond between us that could never be broken. We were best friends, lovers, man and wife, and two hearts intertwined in the divine goodness of life here.

"I could never see her enough. The sound of her voice was enough to melt away any troubling thoughts I had. No load was too great for me with Celia at my side.

"The night we were married, we waited until everyone had gone home and then went back to the falls. There was a full moon shining down on the Nantahala, bathing everything in sight with a form of mystical pale blue light. If there ever was a dream, this night was the one.

"We had only intended to stay for a short while, but it was more than a heart could bear to leave the falls. Our first night together was spent making love and holding each other close by the bed of the falls. When the sun rose from behind the mountains the next morning, we both found it hard to believe we would be together forever.

"I wrapped the blanket around her shoulders and held her close to me there by the falls, until hunger forced us to come back home. A precious smile stayed upon her lips for days to come. We prepared breakfast together that morning. It was the only time in our marriage she ever allowed it. She believed she should always be the one to prepare meals for me. When breakfast was ready, I loaded everything onto a tray and told her to follow me upstairs. She was under the impression we were going to eat in our new bed.

"The surprise was built just for her. I opened the door to the room by the widow's walk and sat the tray on a small table by the window. I was able to see the look of wonderment in her eyes and then small teardrops in the corners. I told her this was her room, and no other should ever be here unless she invited them. She disputed my words and told me the room was ours and was forbidden to anybody else. As usual, I did not argue with her and honored her wishes. You were the first to enter the room since Celia left.

"The portrait of her was painted by an artist in Asheville. She saw it only once.

"She always slept with her head on my shoulder. Sometimes I wonder why she ever bought pillows for the bed.

She demanded things of herself. Always adamant about the manner in which things were done within the house. Never touch the curtains—that was a sure way of getting your head handed to you. Did I say she smiled a lot? Yes, of course, but she also had a fine Irish temper that reared its head on occasion. She was not perfect, Lena, but to me she could do no wrong.

"I tried to do little things to make life easier for her in those days. These were hard times and many things were difficult to come by. Whenever I found some pretty material for dresses, I tried everything possible to get it for her. The third day of our marriage, we were walking down Cemetery Lane, headed for the church picnic. Celia was talking to me about a small dog she had seen at the preacher's house the Sunday afternoon before. I listened and wondered when she would have time for a pet. She reminded me of a butterfly, always fluttering from flower to flower.

"On Monday I told her I may be late and not to hold supper for me. She waited regardless of what I said, and we both ate a warm supper. That is, I ate a warm supper. She was too busy crooning over the small white feist dog I brought home with me. I never told her what the animal cost me, and she did not ask. That in itself was an unusual occurrence.

"Celia had a new dog, and the preacher had a new man to baptize on Sunday. He said I would be a fine addition to the master's flock. Of course, that obligated me to show up at church every Sunday also. Whenever a member of the church was in need, I usually received word to come and help. That was the most expensive dog I have ever owned in my life!

"Everywhere she went this little dog was always close by. Celia made a bed for the dog and kept it by the kitchen door. She taught him simple tricks and smothered the poor thing with more love than any man could ever conceive. I always came first, but the dog was no less my equal. She taught me a lot about life during those times. Things I had taken for granted came to me in a new light. It was an awakening of the spirit within me. She knew the balance of nature and kept it close to her. Sometimes, when I would stand by the river and watch her working with her flowers, I could almost swear the flowers knew what she said to them. To this day I have never seen flowers and trees flourish as well as they did with her touch.

"I never worried about anything when it came down to the inside of the house. She scrubbed the floors and kept the entire house spotless. If you found any dust, it was purely by accident. Celia sewed each and every curtain, bedspread, and pillowcase with her own hands. She purchased very little from the local stores.

"In the evenings of summer, I would come home from the mill and work in the vegetable garden. After supper was said and done, she would join me, working alongside of me until it became too dark to see properly. We would go and sit on the porch for a time and rest. We had electricity, which was a rarity for this part of the mountains at that time. I had all of this installed before the great crash. We used it very little because of the cost. Sometimes we disagreed on the use of it, and Celia usually won the argument. She was fond of candlelight. In her words, 'Candlelight is a comfort to me, and I would like to use it as often as I can.'

"I cannot count the number of nights I listened to her talk of worldly matters she had read about while I laid my head in her lap. Her soft voice was so pleasing to my ears that it was difficult to keep from sleeping. But I didn't. I hung on to every word she spoke, storing them for the times when I had to be away from her.

"On warm summer nights we slept by the widow's walk, where a soft breeze was always there to be enjoyed. I would watch her sleeping at times and thank the Lord for having her by my side. Some nights I couldn't sleep or had other matters on my mind. On these nights, I just held her close and tried to keep her safe.

"On occasion we had her parents to come and eat with us. Except for the holidays, it would be just them. On the holidays, we had every family member she could muster and a few good friends also. It was a grand time for her. The ladies all gathered around and cooked their finest dishes for all to enjoy. I must say Celia's apple cake could not be beaten. I usually was able to trade for some beef on Christmas; if not, we made do with wild turkey and some pork. The hogs I had raised myself. I tried to keep enough meat to store and to trade for living through the winter months.

"Celia canned vegetables and made preserves and jellies. I loved everything she fixed for me. I can honestly say she never ruined anything she cooked. Our first Christmas together, Celia and her father surprised me with a new rifle for hunting. It was new to me, in any case. It had originally belonged to her uncle. It was a fine gun and very accurate. I have placed a lot of meat on my table with that rifle. I shared my good fortune with members of my family.

"I could not have been granted a more peaceful time in my life than when I shared it with her. Sometimes I think back on those days and wonder how we could have been so happy. Times became much better and we started gathering more money. Before the end of the year, my mill was producing lumber for three government contracts. An extension of railroad tracks was placed in our lumberyard for shipping the wood by rail. Everything in my life escalated from that point on.

"Celia could hardly believe our good fortune, nor could I for that matter. The money started coming to us when we started talking about having children of our own. We tried our best, but she was not able to conceive. After the tears dried, we understood some things were not meant to be and accepted the facts. We looked into the possibility of adopting a child, but all the government wanted to do was foster some of the children. Celia did not feel this was acceptable and refused to have anything to do with it. She felt a child should have a permanent home where they could be loved and spoiled. I can agree with her on that.

"There were many times I saw the look in her eyes when a precious little girl would be seen in a store or walking down the street holding her mother's hand. It was the one thing I had no control over whatsoever. My hands were tied.

"I loved walking through these hills while holding her hand. It made me feel like a giant among men. I was her knight in shining armor and held the hand of the fairest princess of them all. Needless to say, life is not a fairy tale. The brothers

Grimm wrote fairy tales for the pleasure of children. If you will read them as an adult, you will quickly discover a villain in every story who frightens you more than a child could ever fathom."

Edward straightened himself in the chair and turned toward Lena. She could see he was hurting and decided not to press him further. There were few words that would come to her mind to try to ease him from the burden of these precious memories. "Edward, I think we should go home for today and get some rest. I can come tomorrow, but this time I'm buying lunch. Deal?"

Edward nodded his agreement, and they sat in silence listening to the rushing of the waters close by. Lena stayed with him until he shakily lifted himself from his chair and went inside to call Betty.

Within minutes, Betty pulled into the yard, and Edward found his seat beside her. With a small wave and a nod, they turned and headed down the path for home. Lena stood waving to the both of them and almost wished she had never made the deal with Edward. It was painful to him, and this burden was all on her shoulders.

Micheal Rivers

Chapter Nine

Lena sat fully awake through the night. In her mind she kept playing a scene over and over within her deepest thoughts. She heard the screeching of Gerald's secretary's voice and her husband defending her. All of this within the confines of her own home, where the secretary was little more than an intruder. Her husband would never know how difficult it was to see another woman wearing her clothes and jewelry. Her eyebrows furrowed, and she growled her contempt for them both.

Rising from her chair, she grabbed her cigarettes and stepped out onto the rear deck of the cabin. The full moon rode high in the Appalachian sky, lighting her way. She had brought a blanket with her from the bedroom and covered her legs as she sat on the deck lounge. Something had to be done very soon if she was to hold on to the little bit of dignity she had left to her.

Suddenly she smiled to herself. A single thought crossed her mind in a flash of genius. Lena knew she had taken everything he had shoveled her way for many years and never made a fuss. She was confident in the knowledge that he would never believe she would retaliate for his behavior. The secret would be to have everything in place for the time she would drop the hammer and end his ways once and for all. A divorce was not in question for now. She wanted to make his life as miserable as he had made hers.

Looking out over the mountains in the early morning sky, she began to laugh deliriously. *Sweet revenge will be the delight of my life!*

The sun rose over the mountains, beginning a new day for her, and she was famished. She cooked everything she liked best for breakfast and then showered for the day. Stepping from the shower, she could hear her phone ringing. Thinking it may be important, she raced to answer it before the caller could hang up. Breathlessly, she answered the phone with a brisk hello.

The voice on the other end of line was Gerald. Lena's smiled passed quickly from her face. "You seem to be up early today, Gerald. Is there a problem?"

Gerald's voice sounded distant. "No, no problem. I just called to tell you I would be out of town the rest of the week so you would not call an empty house."

Lena smiled to herself. "Is it another trip to London, or where?" she asked pensively.

Gerald ignored her tone of voice and continued. "I have to be in Spain to bid on a new steel contract. I should be back by next Thursday. I thought you may want to stay at the cabin until I returned."

Lena almost choked trying to hold back her laughter. "Actually, I thought I would come home tomorrow and stay for a while. I can only take these mountains in small quantities."

Silence reigned on the other end of the line. Finally, Gerald spoke. "Do as you wish, but I will not be here."

Lena thought quickly. "Gerald, I just changed my mind. I believe I will fly to Chicago and spend a few days there. I haven't been in a while, and the trip may do me good."

When she finished speaking, Gerald continued, with the sound of relief in his words. "So I can expect you to be home the following Saturday, is that correct?"

Lena checked her pocket calendar and smiled. "Yes, Gerald, I will see you then."

She had barely finished speaking when she heard the other end of the line go silent. He had hung up the phone without so much as good-bye. Placing the phone back into the cradle, Lena rose from the chair and finished getting dressed. Her next move was to call Edward and tell him she had to return home for a few days and take care of some business. He understood and advised her to be careful. She told him Gerald was traveling out of the country and would not be there. This seemed to satisfy Edward, and he bid her good-bye.

She packed her clothes and hurried to the airport, hoping to catch an early flight. She wanted to be there before Gerald left for his trip. It would be interesting to see if he was to have company on his flight. Unless she missed her guess, there would be someone with him. Lately there always was.

Her flight lasted barely an hour. Lena rented a car and drove to her home. Gerald's car sat in the drive alone, and there was no sign of anyone there but him. Parking close to the corner of the street, she sat and watched the house. Gerald left the house alone and did not have any luggage with him. Smiling to herself, she wondered if he had left someone in the house to wait for his return.

Turning her head as he drove by and trying hard not to be seen, she watched him drive out of sight. Starting the engine, she pulled the gearshift into drive and parked just past her house on the street. Lena crossed the street and walked across her lawn and onto the patio by the back door. As quietly as she possibly could, she unlocked the door and entered the kitchen. Her housekeeper spotted her and almost spoke. She noticed Lena shushed her, attempting to keep her quiet concerning Lena's return.

The housekeeper nodded that she understood and pointed upstairs with a frown on her face. Lena slid quietly down the hallway and walked boldly up the stairs. The smell of a strange perfume greeted her as she neared her bedroom door. The rush of anger swelled within her. With little effort, she opened the bedroom door and saw another woman lying in her bed, fast asleep. The temptation to snatch her out of the bed was tremendous.

Carefully she closed the door and returned downstairs. She told her housekeeper not to say anything about her being there and that she would return soon. Grinning, the housekeeper watched Lena as she left the house and went back to her car.

The time to exact revenge was now, and she was not about to let an opportunity pass so easily. Driving past the federal building, she found a place to park and exited her car. She entered the building directly across the street and walked to the reception desk.

"Can I help you?" the security guard asked.

Lena smiled sweetly. "Yes, I would like to see Charles Messer. I don't have an appointment, but I can assure you he will be happy to see me."

The security guard eyed her curiously and picked up the phone. "I have a Mrs. Lena Leicester here at the front desk to see Mr. Messer." Nodding his head and hanging up the phone, he smiled benignly. "He is located on the third floor, second office on the left."

Lena thanked him politely and headed for the elevator. This would be money well spent, and Charles owed her a favor. Finding the office, she entered the door and introduced herself to the secretary. Immediately she rose and escorted her into Messer's office. Looking about her, Lena could see Charles was coming up in the world. Everything in the office was nothing but first-class.

Charles stood from behind his desk and greeted her warmly. "Lena, it's been a long time since we last saw each other. With you showing up here at the office, it must be something important." He offered her a chair and sat back down behind his desk. "How can I help you today?"

Lena frowned slightly and began her story, and Charles listened intently, trying to catch every word. "My husband has gotten himself another woman. There may be several, I'm not sure. The reason I am here is I need your former talents to wreak havoc on that bastard's life."

Charles laughed. "I was wondering when you were going to get tired of his crap and come see me."

"I am here now, and that is what counts. Money is not a problem as far as your rates are concerned, and anything you need you shall have. My housekeeper will be more than happy to assist you in any area you need in the house. Her discretion is never in question.

"What you find may or may not be used in a divorce case, but I can and will make his life a living hell until I am satisfied."

Charles spoke evenly. "What would you like for me to do?"

Lena leaned forward and rested her arm on the edge of his desk. "At this moment, there is a woman sleeping in my bed. I believe she will be there for at least a week. That is when Gerald is expecting me to come home. I want video, photographs, audio, and anything else you can dig up for me to put him in his place once and for all. He will not ask for a divorce because he would be out of a job and probably have no place to stay. He told me he was flying to Spain this morning and asked me to stay at the cabin. I told him I was going to Chicago for a few days; either way, he is expecting me there the following Saturday after his return."

"Is he on his way to Spain now?" he asked.

"No! I was watching the house, and he never went to the airport," she stated.

"Okay, I will hang out my shingle and tell everybody I am going on vacation. We'll work from there. I will need to get some of the boys together so we can keep tabs on your super-stud."

"What do you want me to do in the meantime?" Lena asked.

"Go back to the cabin and stay clear of this place until I give you a report of some kind. It shouldn't take long to hang him out to dry."

Lena sat back with a sigh of relief. "You have no idea how much I appreciate you doing this for me."

Charles laughed heartily. "You should have married me, and we wouldn't be doing this right now."

Lena snickered. "Charles, you and I both know you would be in prison for strangling my mother."

Shaking his head and remembering her mother, he smiled again. "You're right about that. Maybe you'll give me a chance when you drop the dead weight you are married to now."

"We shall see, Charles. But for now, I need his head on a platter."

Lena left the office and found her car. She called her housekeeper and filled her in on all the details. Without a second thought, she drove back to the airport and caught a flight back to her mountain home.

Edward was close to wearing a path in the carpeting from pacing the floor of his living room. Betty had tried her best to calm him, but he was worried for the safety of his friend. Glancing at the clock, he wondered why he had not heard anything from her.

Betty sat by the phone waiting for a call from Lena. "Mr. Edward, do you think that man has done something to her?"

Edward shook his head. "I have no idea, Betty. He needs to pray he never does. I am too old to take care of him myself, but I have enough money to lay him in the ground and nobody be the wiser for it."

Betty drew back slightly in her chair. "Do you really mean that, Mr. Edward?"

Edward whirled in his tracks. "By the grace of God, I would have it done before the sun set on his sorry carcass."

Suddenly the ringing of the phone blasted the silence that had fallen between them. Betty grabbed the phone and spoke a few words, then hung the phone back in the receiver slowly.

"That was your friend. She is all right and will be at the old house tomorrow afternoon. She said to tell you not to worry, she is safe and sound."

Edward breathed a sigh of relief and headed for the front porch. Betty sat in her chair and listened as she heard Edward humming the tune of a favored song from church.

The next morning Edward arrived at the house early, waiting for some news from Lena. He did not wait long before he saw her walking up the lane and wearing her familiar smile. After they greeted each other, Edward asked, "Did he give you any problem?"

Lena laughed easily. "Oh no, we didn't even speak. Let's not dwell on something as mundane as my husband's actions. Why don't we just enjoy the day and let it be done."

Edward nodded and sat down in his chair. He was breathing heavily and seemed just a touch from being himself. Lena was worried about him. Lately, he was noticeably slowing down in every move he made. The spark of life she had seen in him when they first met was waning like the tide.

"I think today I will let you take the reins and talk to me for a change. That is, if you don't mind."

Lena patted his hand and assured him it was all right. "Shortly after I married Gerald, we found a wonderful house that I fell in love with the minute I passed through the front door. It is a French Colonial–style house in the suburbs of Richmond. My father gave us the down payment for the house without blinking an eye.

"My mother could hardly stand the pressure of not being able to help decorate the rooms. When I told her I wanted to do this myself, she patted my head like the family dog and sent me a professional decorator as a wedding gift. Gerald was happy at least. He puffed out his chest and took on the role of royalty whenever someone came to call.

"A few times I felt like he was not going to introduce me to his new friends. The first time we entertained guests, he made me feel like the maid instead of his wife. I do believe the couple noticed this because I never saw them again.

"He would hold me and kiss me gently while professing his love. This happened only in the privacy of our home, or when there was no chance of anyone seeing us. I cannot count the number of days I was berated for daring to set foot into his library. This room even had a private phone number apart from the rest of the house. If that phone rang, the door was immediately closed and the low voices began.

"He expected everything in the house to be spotless. He would not wear the same suit more than two, maybe three, times before it was replaced by a new one. You have to believe me, he paid handsome prices for his clothes. I really should say at my father's expense. It must have been fine, because my father always complimented him on his taste in suits.

"The first year after we were married, I decided I was going to trade my car for a newer model. The company was providing him with a new Mercedes or whatever he wanted at the time. I did not need anything fancy or expensive, so I went to the local car dealer and bought what I wanted.

"The next morning, after the rage of the century, he informed me that piece of junk would never be seen in his driveway. He returned the car and gave me one of his choosing. Gerald told me I was to drive this car and never to buy anything else behind his back.

"To bring his point home, he tried to have my name stricken from our bank account. This was the only time my mother ever stepped in and told him how the marriage was going to work. She then came to me and blessed me out for not standing up to him. How can you stand up when both sides are knocking you back down at the same time?

"I must admit, my father was not at all pleased at that bit of news either. It made little difference, because Gerald took his displeasure of the incident out on me every chance he could.

"This was when he became mentally abusive. We were going to a corporate party on the Fourth of July where my father had some very influential guests expected. I got dressed and was standing in the kitchen with a glass of wine when Gerald came in. He bumped into me, spilling the wine all over the new gown. He said I was the clumsiest person he had ever seen and screamed at me because we were going to be late.

"I had to change into one of my old dresses and go to the celebration. My mother noticed right away I was wearing something she had seen before and scolded me for not getting something special for the occasion. This was when Gerald offered his services and told her I was clumsy and spilled wine all over the new dress. He made sure anyone close to us could hear him.

"This was not the first, nor the last, time he tried to embarrass me in front of others. I have to admit, he was very good at it. He told me how to dress, when to dress, and where we would dine on a regular basis.

"After he began to tire of me, he started working late and traveling quite a bit. That was when we bought the cabin here. He traveled and I started coming here. He has been here just enough to let the locals know I have a husband and he is a pompous ass.

"Anything I do is improper, an embarrassment, or sheer lunacy. I do expect him to begin walking on water at any time.

"I believe he wants to stay with me until I receive my inheritance when my father passes, and then he can do whatever he wants without fear of reprisal."

Edward shook his head in sorrow. "I had no idea things were as bad as they are for you. I can see he will not change until something drastic happens and forces the change in him. I saw men like him when I was still in business. They seem to have little regard for those who care about them.

"From what you have told me, you have a beautiful house in Richmond, but that doesn't make it a home. I knew of women others had labeled as gold diggers. I am here to tell you that when some men get the scent of money in their nostrils, they are worse than any woman ever dared to be. He cannot be trusted in any form. Are you going to do anything about this situation?"

Lena shrugged her shoulders. "There is not a lot I can do. I feel I cannot live with the stigma of being divorced. Where I came from, this is simply not done. I am also Catholic, so I have to stay within my bounds."

"Lena, you cannot keep staying in a situation where you have no life to speak of. Happiness is much more than a feeling. Listen to an old man who knows. For the love of God, get your life under control before it destroys what time you have left on this earth."

Lena looked into his eyes and smiled sweetly. "At least I know you care, and that means a lot to me."

Edward swore. "I have said all on the matter I should have. The end of the story has to come from you. Think long and hard. Try to make sure whatever you do is the right thing for you."

Lena nodded slowly and turned her eyes to stare off over the ridge. It was wonderful here, and she knew if anyone ever cared what happened to her, it was Edward.

Edward knew in his heart something had to be done. He had grieved for his Celia his entire life and knew happiness was a fleeting thing. This young heart sitting next to him should never have to endure the pain of living without something as precious as the gift of happiness.

"Lena, when you look at this house, what comes to your mind?"

It was an awkward question, but it was a question that deserved an answer. "I see a home. Not just any home, but a home in a magical place. Time stands still here. The worries of the world seem so far away when you are sitting here listening to the sounds of the meadow around you. The soothing sounds of the river lull you into a sense of well-being. This is a house true love built, I have no doubt.

"You have a home to be proud of. I have seen castles, mansions, and a palace or two. You will have to believe me when I tell you they can never compare with what I have felt and seen here."

Edward smiled to himself and bent to light his pipe. His decision was made as to what he wanted to do with the remainder of his time. "Lena, you have no idea what a wonderful gift you have just given me. I did not know what I was going to do with the time I have left to live. With your words, I know without a doubt what I want to do."

Lena giggled. "What would that be, sir, if I may ask?"

Edward drew deeply on his pipe and smiled. "When you come here tomorrow, you will know.

Chapter Ten

Edward returned to the bungalow that afternoon with a spring in his step and a smile on his face. Betty was having trouble trying to figure out whether he had been drinking or he just had found a renewed energy.

Betty could stand the suspense no longer and pounced on Edward. "Okay, old man, you want to tell me what you are up to, or do I have to drag it out of you?"

Edward beamed with joy. "Yes, I do want to tell you. Starting tomorrow, I want you to pack anything you want to take to my house. Whatever you want to leave here is fine, but I will be spending the rest of my days in my house."

Edward held his hand to stop Betty from saying anything. "I know what the doctor said, and I am fully aware of what my friends think and feel. This is just for a short time, the time I have left to me. If anything happens to me, so be it. The fact of the matter is I will spend the rest of my days in my own house, sleeping in my own bed."

Betty stood before him with her mouth hanging open. She could not understand what had caused the change in him, but she liked it. This was the Edward Caulfield she was accustomed to!

Edward turned and smiled. "If you are going to stay with me, I would suggest you get packing before I fall over dead. By the look on your face, you probably think I have been dancing with the devil. I'm here to tell you it ain't so. I just decided I am finished doing what makes everybody else happy, and I am going to start living my own life."

Betty stepped off, saying nothing. Under her breath, she whispered aloud. "The old fart has finally lost what little mind he had left."

Betty assured Edward she would start packing his things and have them at the house by the end of the following day. Edward thanked her and asked her if staying there would be a problem for her. She said it was no problem, and yet she wondered what she would do should anything happen to

Edward. It was a time when all things must be left in the hands of the Lord, in her opinion.

When the sun rose from behind the mountains the following morning, Edward was already making his way to the coffee shop. He ordered a big breakfast and waited to see if any of his old friends would come in so he could talk with them as he did years ago.

Mickey Fisher was a good friend and an old fishing buddy. When Mickey fell ill, Edward did not see him for almost two years. His friend did not allow anyone to visit, and his daughter made certain his wishes were followed to the letter.

The door of the coffee shop swung open slowly, and Edward looked up to see who was coming through the door. He recognized Mickey at once and started to rise. Mickey's daughter whispered something in his ear, and Mickey nodded shakily and smiled. Within minutes, Mickey and Edward were talking to each other as if it were yesterday.

The next hour was filled with old fishing and hunting stories that both would never forget. When the door of the coffee shop opened once more, a familiar face walked to their booth and greeted them. The man standing before them was Freddy Wilkes's eldest son. He bore the news no friend ever wanted to hear.

"Gentlemen, I came down here hoping to find you. Daddy died this morning, and Momma wanted me to let you know instead of you reading it in the paper."

Edward drew in a sharp breath. "Can I ask what happened?"

The young man sighed heavily. "He got dressed to come here and stepped out of the front door. He made it as far as the mailbox and then his heart gave out on him. Doc Early said his heart just quit, plain and simple."

The three of them talked briefly, and then the young man went about his business. Mickey turned to Edward with sadness in his voice. "Do you realize, Edward, we are the only two left out of the old crowd that hung around together?"

Edward nodded and smiled. "I am sorry he has gone, but I don't plan on being the next in line."

Mickey laughed and excused himself from the table. His daughter held his arm to steady him, and they said their good-byes.

Edward watched as Mickey hobbled out of the door in the care of his daughter. Edward had been lucky all these years, and it was rare he suffered from anything other than a common cold. He refused to give in to sickness, although there were times he just wanted to lie down and let his body do whatever it wished to him.

Edward laid the tip for the waitress on the table next to his cup and headed for the door. Once on the street, the thought of losing Freddy hit him hard. He stopped at the corner and wiped the tears from his eyes with his handkerchief. It was a time when his own mortality seemed to stare him in the face.

Shaking off his sadness, he began to walk toward his house by the river. Soon, his thoughts were focused on his new venture. He was going home. His house by the river would always be the only place he wanted to be.

Arriving at the house, he stepped shakily onto the porch and unlocked the front door. Stepping inside, he walked from room to room taking the furniture covers and placing them in a pile next to the door of each room. He kicked himself for ever being talked into leaving for the bungalow in town.

A familiar voice called to him from the back porch. "Is anybody home?"

Edward snickered and called back, "Nobody but us chickens. Come on in if you have the time."

Lena stepped through the door and saw what Edward had been doing. "Is this cleaning day? I would have brought some different clothes if I had known."

Edward stood erect. "I told you yesterday that I had made a decision. This is it. I am coming back home for good. The next time I leave this house will be when they carry me out."

Lena could not help but notice the change in him. A house that was once a shrine and not to be touched was now open and welcoming to anyone. There was a new dawning in the life of Edward Caulfield, and Lena was happy to be a part of it.

The days began to pass, and Lena sat with Edward, speaking of every topic under the sun. They laughed and enjoyed their time together. Betty soon became like a second mother to her and tutored Lena in the joys of living. Edward watched Lena and Betty in the garden working the flowers planted. It was a sharp contrast between the two cultures colliding in a place where heritage was king and visitors were always just that. Betty enjoyed teaching Lena the things a school could never come close to giving her. With the touch of a master chef, Lena soon produced a biscuit that would make a country boy sing. As for Betty, she was unable to keep from smiling just at the sight of seeing Lena's face light at her success.

The time spent together gave an outsider the impression this was a close family with ties that could never be broken. Edward made his way down by the river and relaxed in his chair. Betty watched him from the window and grinned. *If there ever was a heaven, that old coot is certainly sitting on its front porch.*

Taking off her apron, she poured two glasses of iced tea and carried them down to sit with Edward. Edward laughed to himself at the sight of Betty almost waddling across the yard as she headed toward him. "Be careful with those glasses there, Garbo, I wouldn't want you to spill any of it."

Betty shook her head and flopped breathlessly in the chair beside him. "For an educated man, you sure ain't got the sense God gave a goat. Everybody knows I ain't any Greta Garbo. But I am a damn close second to Andy Devine." Betty laughed uproariously at her joke and then continued on. "Mr. Edward, the day you decided to come back here was the best thing you ever did in your life. I have never seen you look so good."

Edward pulled his hat down low over his eyes to shade them from the afternoon sun. He sat in silence wondering why he had not done this before.

Betty interrupted his thoughts, talking as if speaking to herself. "I was wrong about that little girl for a while. I figured she was up to something. I apologize to you for that. I hope you can see she has a lot of Miss Celia in her, that one does. You cain't help but light up at the sight of her. You have given me enough stories about Miss Celia that I can almost tell you word for word what she was like. I seen you light up at supper the other night when she throwed those biscuits on the table. It was good to my soul to see you think I done it."

Edward turned and cocked his head at her. "I would have sworn that was your cooking, Betty. The both of you fooled me for a change."

Betty grinned slyly. "Gettin' something past you ain't so hard these days. I do worry 'bout you, I can say that for sure."

"You are right, Betty. Lena is a lot like Celia in so many ways. When we first started talking here at the house, I had no idea she was so much like her. Life has a funny way of bringing back memories you can't recall when you feel you need to. She is easy to talk to and makes you think."

"You have to give the girl credit, she is gaining a mind of her own. I hate to say it, but I think you might have something to do with that. Don't ruin a good thing, you old coot. I see how you look at her. Anybody that didn't know better would swear she was your child."

Edward beamed with pride. "Before you know it, she might stick her foot up her husband's ass just to please her momma."

"I want to be there for the event when it does happen," Betty crowed.

Edward reached for his tea and sipped slowly. Betty sat watching him with a sly grin stretching across her face. Edward sat the glass back onto the table, smacking his lips. "Betty, this is some of the best tea you have made in ages."

"I didn't make that tea—Lena did. She put too much sugar in it. Before you get ahead of yourself, don't go thinkin' you gonna put me to the street and have her fixin' your supper for ya."

Edward stared at Betty and winked. "Now, Betty, how can you think that way? I couldn't make it without you. Besides, I had dreams of taking you fishing so I would have somebody to paddle the boat. I understand you can bait a hook with the best of them."

Betty rose to her feet and shook her fist at Edward. "It's time for me to git back in the house. Think hard on this, you old buzzard. If you and I go fishin', the only worm on the hook will wind up being yours!"

Edward grinned broadly as he watched Betty walk back toward the front porch. It was a joy to see her get riled up and strut like a pissed-off rooster.

Soon the silence of the evening overshadowed all of the day's ventures, and Edward sat alone beneath his tree. A pang of longing for the sight of his Celia pierced his heart—a sight that was not to be.

Betty had gotten everything moved in with her usual efficiency. The transition would have made the professionals proud. She did not accept people easily, and yet Betty had made a bond with Lena. It was a pleasing thought. Later in the evening, Lena stopped by to help Betty finish any chores that were left to do. Edward overheard Betty telling Lena in the kitchen that she was safe as long as she stayed with them. He could hear the muffled sounds of someone crying. He slipped out of the front door and made his way to the garage, giving them time to talk with each other.

The times when we have someone to hold on to are few and the moments are precious. This was a time for the ladies. Regardless of looks or education, Betty was a thoroughbred mountain girl and every inch a lady. Edward respected her, and at times she seemed to hold the wisdom of kings. He was right: life would have been very different without Betty to help him.

Lena had left without seeing him. Edward assured himself she needed time alone. Looking up at the sky, he saw some very dark clouds building. There was a storm brewing, and he was glad Lena had left when she did. A harsh wind suddenly came from the east and forced Edward back into the house. The storm was almost on top of them now, and he wanted to prepare for when they would lose power. He reached into a closet in the kitchen and pulled down the extra oil lamps, setting them in areas about the house.

Betty gathered wood for a fire to drive out the damp air. Just as she closed the back door, lightning skated across the skies, followed by a horrific clap of thunder. "This is going to be a bad one, Mr. Edward. Do want anything to eat before we sit down?" she asked.

Edward shook his head. "I would rather you stay away from the kitchen until this storm blows over."

Betty agreed, and the two of sat before a warming fire watching the lightning light up the room with every flash. Rain fell in torrents about the house, and the river swelled to its peak. Edward knew there may be damage to his property after a storm like this, but there was nothing that could be done until it was over.

The fear in Betty's eyes was evident. Edward tried to calm her as best he knew how. She was a tough woman, but this storm frightened her badly. Light conversation did nothing to ease her fears. A thought crossed Edward's mind, and he went into his old office and picked up his banjo. Sometimes music can take you away from your troubles. During this time of trouble, music was a blessing.

.

Chapter Eleven

The aftermath of the storm revealed not as much damage as Edward had proposed it would. Tree limbs lay strewn about and a few shingles were missing from the rooftop. Two boards had been pulled from the porch and lay at odd angles to each other. The river still ran deep, overlapping its banks. Edward felt grateful there was no more damage than what he was witnessing now. Edward placed a call to Buck and asked him if he would stop by and take a look at his house for him in the chance he had missed something important. Buck readily agreed and was at Edward's house by noon.

Betty and Lena stood by the tree watching the men talking when Betty crossed her arms and stared straight ahead. "That old man is up to something. I know by the way he is talking to Buck. I wish I could hear what he's tellin' him. You never know what that old coot is gonna do next. I think the world of him, but he drives me crazy at times."

Lena laughed. "Maybe he is cooking up something just for the sake of making you feel that way. He loves you like family. You should know that by now. I am like you right now. I want to know what he is doing. It doesn't take this long to talk about replacing a few busted shingles."

Buck climbed back into his truck and drove slowly down the path, headed for town. Edward never said a word concerning his conversation with Buck and ignored any questions the two women raised.

Two more days passed with the women wondering what Edward had done. He walked about whistling nameless tunes and watching the two of them squirm with curiosity. The following morning they were surprised when Buck and two other men pulled into the driveway and unloaded their tools. The minor repairs finished, Buck and his crew gathered their brushes and began to scrape and paint the house. Betty could not believe her eyes. Edward had waited all of these years, never bothering to paint the house. He fairly danced as he watched the house transform from its former self back into a vision of beauty.

Sitting by the tree and sipping on a jar of Nantahala's finest, Edward could not deny his look of satisfaction. Lena strolled over and sat in the grass beneath the tree. "I see you are making progress nicely. Your house is looking like a fairy tale again."

Edward nodded.

"You are a rare breed, Caulfield. I must insist you have a word with my publicist. We can have you on Leno or one of the other shows when you have a hole in your schedule."

Edward shook his head, wondering. "You, dear lady, have been spending entirely too much time with Betty. It is starting to rub off on you. I wanted my house to shine in the light of my world; that is, if you and the Mona Lisa in there have no objections."

Lena snickered. "Yes, we have been discussing you. No, I will not tell you what has been said. As far as any objections are concerned, I think you are doing the proper thing. The house looks magnificent. Now, you have procrastinated long enough. You have to get back to our bargain. You may begin at any time."

"I can see you have a mean streak in you I never noticed before. We have time to tell the story. You don't have to be in a rush."

"I am in no hurry, but my curiosity is killing me, especially after seeing such a change in your demeanor. As you said to me, a deal is a deal, so get on with it."

"My Lord, you are starting to sound just like Betty," he snapped.

From behind them they heard Betty speak up. "That is a good thing, you old fart. You had me to yourself for too long. Now you have to deal with both of us."

Edward turned in his chair. "Lena, do you see what you have started here? I will not tolerate this absurd treachery from the hired help!"

Betty sat down in the chair next to him and grinned. "You have to keep your promise to this little girl. I believe I will sit here until you do. That is my way of saying I want to hear this story too."

Edward was outnumbered and he knew it. There was some doubt as to whether he wanted Betty to hear what was in his heart. Still, he had been with Betty for a long time and was sure she was aware of many of his feelings. There were so many memories he wanted to share. Where to begin was the problem for him. Some of the memories he would hold sacred in his heart, and they would stay with him until he was cold in his grave. Others had earned the right to be shared so others would understand who he was.

"I think I will begin with her first birthday after we were married. It was a very special day for her. I took the day off from work and watched her go into an Irish tantrum over people wanting to say I was getting lazy. I explained to her that when the boss takes a day off, the only person who had the right to complain was her and it would do her no good. She accepted that explanation but was not thoroughly convinced it was correct.

"We ate a late breakfast, and I told her to get dressed because we were going for a ride. This could not have pleased her any better. The chance to socialize was always at the top of her list. I went out to the stable and prepared the carriage we liked to use for church and brought it around the front of the house. You may say the carriage was outdated for those days, but my lady loved it. She always liked the way things were done before her time. I never denied her anything.

"She always rode with her head held high and a smile on her face. We took the back roads over the mountains into Jackson County. It was a very pleasant day with mild temperatures and just a hint of sweet grass in the air. The truth be told, I can still see us riding down the narrow roads now. That old horse of mine never broke stride, no matter how steep the hills became.

"Close to noon we stopped on a hilltop and had lunch from a basket she had prepared before we left. I had a lot of difficulty keeping my eyes off her. She was like something from a dream sitting next to me. If a portrait could have been painted of her resting on the hill, it would still not have captured what I was seeing. With every breath I fell deeper into love with her.

"The afternoon was passing quickly. She never asked when we were going back home or any of the questions you would expect. She took everything in stride as if she knew what I was doing. I checked my pocket watch and noticed it was nearly three o'clock. I was a bit behind schedule, but she never knew this. Soon I came up on the road to a man's house I had been heading for the whole journey. He came out of house and greeted us, offering something cold to drink. No, it wasn't lemonade, I can assure you. Celia blushed and declined his offer.

"Celia was talking with his wife and their two heads were bobbing like chickens at a corn festival. When I was able to get her attention, she looked up to see a tall chestnut mare standing in the yard.

"Celia could hardly believe her eyes. It had to be the finest horse in the county. She left the porch and approached the horse as if she had known it from a colt. This was when I wished her a happy birthday and handed her the reins. The owner of the horse did not want to sell her, but for need of money he was quick to sell her to me. I received the sweetest hug any man could ever ask for, but she never dropped the reins.

"That night we slept at the boarding house next to the train tracks in Whittier. She rose early the next morning and never stopped for breakfast. We picked up her new horse and tied it to the back of the carriage, and we headed for home. The trip home had to be hard for her. She kept looking back at the mare with a smile that would stretch your face way of shape. I don't think I was able to say very much on that trip home because Celia was busy talking about the horse.

"She named the mare Rosey. I have to admit, the horse loved her almost as much as I did. She loved to ride the mare and offered to let me ride her. I told Celia that Rosey belonged to her and I wanted her to enjoy the mare.

"She had made a cake for her birthday, but by the time we arrived home, the cake was too dry to eat, and it made her cry.

"One of the things I remember most was the sound of her voice and the manner in which she spoke when she told me she loved me. Life passes on each day with new events, and you become complacent. There are so many ways you start to take life for granted. I remember every touch, every kiss, each warm hug, and most of all, lying in each other's arms.

"The things she gave to me were more valuable than all the gold on earth. She never knew how much she meant to me. I have regretted not spending more time with her. She told me she was happy and prayed for a long life together. I laughed at her and said she could never leave me. The look in her eyes that night should have told me to be careful of what I was saying.

"There were times when the workdays drew on longer than I wanted them to. I wanted to come home and be with Celia. A man must make a living to take care of his family. I agree with this. If you think for a bit, you will realize that by doing this you also lose precious time with those you truly love.

"During the third year of our marriage, I knew there was no one man walking the face of the earth as blessed as I was. In the same breath, I felt as though a storm cloud was gathering over my head and there was nothing I could do about it. I explained to you a while back about the tradition of Angel Falls. The spirits did tell me of my life, and by this time I knew they had to be mistaken. The things in this world we don't understand are truly not meant for us to have the knowledge of.

"I came up with an idea to surprise Celia, thinking she would love it. I was right, she was thrilled. I bought a Ford coupe convertible. We drove around the state like we were the only people alive. Gasoline was scarce for a time, but I manage to get gasoline anytime I wanted it. It was one of the advantages of owning a sawmill with government contracts.

"It was the day before our anniversary, and I wanted to do something special for her. I came home from work and told her to pack a few things because we were going to spend the weekend in Asheville to celebrate our anniversary. I wish you could have seen the joy in her eyes. They sparkled like the sun on the waters of the Nantahala.

"We left the next morning and started driving through the mountains for Asheville. I had made arrangements to stay at the finest hotel they had to offer. My plans were to make this a time she would never forget. We danced and held each other in the night. She shopped the local stores and bought a few things for herself and the house.

"I bought a shotgun and some hunting clothes I had seen advertised in a catalogue. We knew life did not get better than what we had now. It was a half day's drive from Asheville to our home, and we should have gotten an earlier start, but we didn't. We stopped in a shop along the way and indulged with some ice cream and cake. This put us another hour later arriving at home.

"The skies were clear when we left the city of Asheville, but soon the sky turned ugly and it began to rain heavily. I stopped by the side of the road and tried to get the convertible top up to keep us dry. Celia and I were already soaked to the skin.

"With the top finally up, we tried the heater on the car in an attempt to dry our clothes. It didn't work, so we were obliged to finish the ride home soaked in rain water beyond belief.

"A few days later Celia began to cough. Just a little in the beginning, and then it progressively grew worse. She didn't want a doctor. Celia said it was just a summer cold and would be gone soon. I came home from work a few days after our return and noticed Celia was not to be seen. She had a habit of waiting for me by the porch when I came home from work.

"Once inside the house, I found her in our bedroom with a high fever and a few droplets of blood on her pillow. I called for the doctor and soothed her brow as best as I knew how. The wait for the doctor seemed to take an eternity. I knew in my heart she had gotten sick from riding home in her wet clothes. I had faith in my doctor and was certain once he was here Celia would get some medicine and be better soon. I never left her side.

"The doctor came and examined her. It felt like he was with her for years. He came out into the hallway and closed the door behind him. I can still feel the touch of his hand on my shoulder."

Edward's voice seemed to be failing him. Lena and Betty could see the glimmer of tears in his eyes. They both sat quietly and tried to let him gain his composure.

"The doctor told me Celia had pneumonia, and it was very serious. He regretted having to tell me, but there was nothing he could do for her. She had waited too long before seeing him. The only thing we could do was wait for her time to end. The rest was in the hands of the Lord.

"In the beginning, I couldn't accept what he was telling me. Once I understood, my heart ached for my Celia. I prayed with everything I had inside of me, but this was to no end of my misery. I spent the remainder of the night beside her as the doctor kept checking her for a possible miracle. I heard her trying to say something and came closer to the bed. With my ear nearly on her lips, I barely heard her tell me she loved me. Two minutes after midnight, my Celia had left me.

"My heart shattered, leaving me with feelings that were unimaginable to anyone but me. The thoughtful words from my friends and people close to me meant nothing. A reason for her being taken from me was never to come, no matter how much I prayed. She is buried in a place just over the ridge behind the house. I can't bring myself to go there because I still will not accept the fact she is gone. It is true, I tell people at times that she is dead, but in my heart she is as alive and vibrant as any woman living today.

"My heart contradicts my mind. This house sat for all these years just as she left it, until I suddenly realized by talking to you I had not heeded my own advice. Happiness is not an illusion and never will be. If you stop and think about the way I have lived my life since the day Celia passed away, I died with her. You made me see I could have been happy living with her memory and the time she gave to me, instead of grieving my life away.

"I can only hope I did not put my burden on others during these years. Betty has stood by me for many years now and knows me better than anyone. I have not been easy to live with, and I know it. As sure as I sit here today, I will not be the man I was. Celia would not have wanted that. There will come a time when I will be with her again, and I am sure we will be together in eternity. Until that time comes, I will do my best to make her proud of me."

Betty sat silently, watching his eyes. She believed he was telling the truth. He had nothing to be ashamed of. Edward had been there to help his fellow man when all others stood in the background. He was a giving man with a passion for others. To hold the torch for Celia was not an easy thing to do in the years since she had died. He was forever faithful to her, and that was no small feat.

"Mr. Edward, you held this house and your heart like a shrine for Miss Celia. I don't see no harm in it. As far as your happiness is concerned, that was all up to you. You gave a lot of things to a lot of people, and it won't never be forgotten in this town. You had the joy of giving—you just couldn't see it."

Lena chimed in, "I would give my right arm for someone to love me as you loved Celia. You should have seen the joy and happiness you were living just by remembering her as you have."

Edward pulled his hat low over his eyes and relighted his pipe. "Say what you wish; the way I lived made misery a second nature for me when I was alone."

Betty reached over and patted him lightly on the knee. "We are going in to fix you some supper. Rest yourself a spell, and I'll call you when we're ready for you."

Edward never acknowledged them as they arose and walked back to the house. He was lost in thought. Buck and his helpers had made progress on the old house, and it was as beautiful as the day it was built. A look of pride shone about him when he saw the old house now.

With little effort his mind had taken him back again to his younger days. He sat watching Celia weeding her flower beds. She stopped and straightened herself, and she smiled and waved to him. Her voice soft and sweet came to him, nearly a whisper. *I have been waiting for you all day. I hope things went well.*

Edward started with a jump. Betty stood in front of him, tapping him on the shoulder. "Your supper is ready. Come on and eat 'fore it gets cold."

Without a word, he rose from his chair and walked with Betty back across the yard to the house. In the kitchen the smell of fresh-baked bread assaulted his sense of smell. He smiled broadly and crowed, "There is nothing like the smell of fresh-baked bread! Let's eat before it gets cold."

Betty snorted. "You need to get your nose fixed. I told you before, I don't know how to make bread. It's biscuits or cornbread, take your pick."

His smile faded quickly and Edward apologized. "You can't blame a man for trying, can you? Thought maybe you would learn how after a while."

Betty fussed around the kitchen, ignoring him. When everyone was seated at the table, Betty looked at Edward and quipped, "It's your turn to say grace, and make sure you don't rush it with company at the table."

Micheal Rivers

Chapter Twelve

The past few days had been very pleasant for Lena. She returned to her cabin to find several messages on her answering machine. Picking up the phone, she returned the call from Charles first.

His gruff voice came on the line after the first ring. "I have been expecting you, how is Chicago?" He laughed uproariously.

"Excellent, best trip I have never taken. Do you have some news for me?" she asked.

Charles cleared his throat. In the background she could hear the shuffle of papers being strewn about. "Yes, it would seem your husband has been a very busy man."

"How busy, dare I ask?"

"The day you left Richmond, he came out of the house with several suitcases and a woman. Her name is Stephanie Mason-Moore. Do you know her?"

"No, that's a new name to me."

"Some of my men went in and wired the house while I followed him. He took a flight to the Caymans. He made reservations for two at a hotel there for three days. That would put him back before you could be at home. This Stephanie Mason-Moore is the niece of the guy who owns Panama Steel. She is a looker for sure, and a lot younger than he is."

"Do you have any idea how long she has been in my house?"

"Yes, your housekeeper said she arrived the night before you unexpectedly popped in."

"What else have you got for me?"

"I checked into his money situation. We have found three more accounts besides the two accounts you already have. He gets the majority of his mail at his office, and the secretary is paying the bills from one of the accounts."

"I know for a fact he has been spending a lot of time with his secretary. That is in more ways than one, I am sure."

"I figured that too from the copies of receipts I have for you."

"Do any of those accounts involve my father's finances?"

"Indeed they do. Gerald goes through the company money like it belongs to him."

"I thought about coming home a day early. What do you think?"

"Stay on your schedule, and I'll meet you at the airport. I have some receipts for your Chicago trip for you. It will cover you in case he is snooping, which I know he already is. He hired a private investigator to track you. These receipts will make a liar out of his investigator. He knows you have been spending a lot of time with the old man. The word is out that he thinks you are after the old man's money, and he wants his share of it."

"What do you believe?"

"I have known you and your family for a long time. I say it is a lot horse crap. Give it some thought and keep your eyes open. Just for the sake of being careful, check the house for surveillance, and I'll send a guy down to make sure."

"Thank you for calling and giving me the update. I'll see you again in a few days."

The line went silent before she could place the receiver back in its cradle. It amazed her, the amount of greed Gerald was capable of having. She hesitated for only a second. Why would Gerald go to the Caymans? He loved a lavish lifestyle with the belles of society at his feet. The Caymans had been too sedate for him before.

She knew he was trying to hide his tracks because of the simple fact they had friends with beautiful homes on the beach that he could have had for the asking. Charles had told her of a private investigator hounding her trail. Gerald was trying to find a way to keep her under his thumb. It was too obvious even for her. It looked like when he found out about Edward, his tiny mind veered into a twilight zone.

The very thought of his actions were revolting. Lena rose from her chair silently and began to inspect every inch of her house. If there were cameras or recording devices in her home, she had to find them.

She found nothing. Charles's man would be able to detect more than she could, so she would just have to wait.

The next day she returned to visit with Edward and Betty. Lena was looking forward to spending time with them. Approaching the house, she noticed Buck and his crew were already working.

Betty stepped out onto the porch and greeted her warmly. Lena noticed Edward was sitting in the chair by the window. In a low voice, Betty told her he was not feeling well today, but he was still looking forward to her visit.

Lena smiled and walked boldly into the living room. "It is a nice day. You should be out by the tree enjoying the shade."

Edward smiled wanly and offered her a chair. "Yes, it is a lovely day, but I am a little out of sorts, so I am holding down this chair while waiting for you."

Lena grinned happily. "I am here, so let the festivities begin."

Betty growled and started for the kitchen. "I think both of you have lost what mind you had."

Edward called after her. "Don't get mad, Garbo. I have invited Brad Pitt for lunch again, and he should be here by noon. You can fix him a chicken leg or something."

Edward placed his finger to his lips, indicating for Lena to be quiet. Suddenly the kitchen door slammed loudly, shaking the frame. "She is a little testy today, so I thought I would help her get to a slow boil."

Lena held her head back, laughing. "You do not give her a break, do you?"

Edward grimaced and cocked his head, looking at her sidelong. "If I give her a break, she will take advantage of my good nature. Knowing her, she will swear I don't love her anymore. What a pity."

Edward stretched his right leg and rubbed vigorously. "Arthritis has cursed me pretty good today. Like that pain in the butt you married. Now it is your turn to sit down and give me your story."

Lena shook her head. "Not a lot to tell. But I will give it a shot. I told you about the wedding and the poor excuse for a honeymoon. The rest of the story should have been written by a horror writer. That, or Benny Hill. Either one would be correct.

"When times began to get really rocky, I tried to be at the cabin as much as possible. That did not always work out. Gerald and I had a disagreement concerning a boat he wanted to purchase. He did not know how to operate a boat that size and would have to hire somebody to run it for him. He stomped out of the house and then called later in the day to let me know he was flying to Texas for a meeting. Naturally, he would be back the following day.

"In the interim, my mother called and demanded I take in an opera with her in New York. She was paying for the trip and already had a dress for me. Like a good child, I accepted and drove to her house. We left from there and drove to the airport.

"The rest of the day went like all days in her company. I tried everything to please her and listened to all her petty complaints about those around her. The limousine picked us up from the hotel at exactly eight o'clock. Mother is fond of the white stretch limousines so she will be easy to spot.

"We were escorted to our seats in the balcony. Nothing but first class all the way! Twenty minutes later, the first of the many screeching violets hit the stage. I listened for a while, but when I became bored I looked around. I recognized a few of my father's friends—one of them was even kind enough to wink at me.

"While inspecting the theater, I perused the seats below us during the second act. Sitting almost directly below us was Gerald and a woman I had never seen. I watched them for a bit and saw where he placed his hand. That was bad enough, but the kiss finished me for good. I excused myself and went back to the hotel feigning illness.

"That was the first time I found him to be a cheat. There were many other times as well. Now, he has taken to bringing his women home with him and sleeping in my bed.

"When I am there, he acts like he is the perfect husband. My mother and father refuse to believe he would do such a thing. According to them, I am imagining things. He has them convinced that I am. My mother actually contrived to have me committed for accusing him of his deeds.

"After I knew I did not stand a chance of my own parents helping me, I decided not to say anything to them about the company money or anything else Gerald was doing. This worked out very well for them, although I still had to live with it. We did the usual holiday dinners, as well as the trips here and there. If Gerald made an excuse not to be there, it was fine. If I bowed out of a simple luncheon, her coven had me roasting on a spit before Washington society.

"For a time the in-vogue situation was to have a chalet in Vale. He bought a large chalet complete with full service. I was surprised he didn't have someone to wipe his mouth for him. We had a party, and I caught him in the den wrapped around an up-and-coming starlet from California. I threw her out and continued talking with our guests. After the party ended, he pushed me out of the house and locked the doors. I was forced to sleep in the car that evening. The closest neighbor was more than a mile away and out of town for the week.

"These are just a few of the minor examples of what he does to me. The fun and games continue at home, so I spend as much time as I can at my cabin.

"I can tell you without a doubt, when my parents are gone, he will take my inheritance and leave me flapping in the wind. Before you say anything, I have already been told by Mother's lawyer he has been placed as executor of the estate with full power. As the old song goes, 'Ain't that a kick in the head?'"

Edward sat staring at Lena. Her future at present was bleak at best. She managed to smile and put up a very good front for people. Edward eased back into his chair and snuggled into the plush seat painfully. "This being the case, what are you going to do when they are gone?"

Lena shrugged. "I will have to take whatever bones are thrown my way and do the best I am able. I am a survivor. I have friends that will help when they can. I will have to stay until he divorces me. It is a fact, with the situation like it is, I can never divorce him."

The two of them sat and talked for the rest of the day, until Edward fell asleep in his chair.

Chapter Thirteen

Edward was not a foolish man. He had learned the ways of the business world and knew the lessons well. He was satisfied with his decisions concerning Betty's future. Somewhere there had to be a solution for the suffering that Lena was enduring in her life. Age was steadily creeping in upon him, and with it, his body no longer seemed to want to cooperate in many ways. Time was of the essence because his time was short by his standards. He prayed each day his mind would still stay sharp enough to know where he was and capable enough to do things for himself.

The morning had started off just as every other morning for the past ten years, but today was different in many respects. When Edward was leaving his home, Betty inquired as to where he was going. Without a word, he slid out of the door and down the steps. He wanted to keep this day unto himself. He needed room to think, and home was not the place.

Edward made his first stop by his doctor's office. Once inside, he did not have long to wait. This was a blessing, considering the worn-out magazines about mothers who did not know how to take care of their children and the best way to care for your hemorrhoids staring him in the face.

The news from his doctor was what he had expected. He thanked him and appreciated the fact there was no charge for the visit. Two doors down, he walked into the office of his lawyer, expecting to be turned away for showing up without an appointment.

The secretary behind the desk greeted Edward with a big smile and many kind words. Within minutes he was sitting in his old friend's office, discussing everything he had on his mind. Nods and grunts came from both sides until an agreement was reached, and then Edward took his leave.

Time had passed quickly and the day was nearly gone. His stomach grumbled at the thought of not having eaten lunch yet. Edward stopped into the coffee shop and grabbed the closest booth to the door. There was a new waitress headed for him whom he had not seen before. Laughing, Edward asked her about her counterpart and saw the young girl frown. "She decided it was a good day to walk out, so she did. You may have to wait a bit because I am tending the shop by myself today."

Edward said he felt sorry for her and let her know her efforts would not go unrewarded. She took his order and hurried off to the kitchen. Edward looked around slowly. There was not a soul he remotely recognized sitting at the tables around him. It was a very lonely feeling knowing your friends were either dead or stuffed away in a nursing home somewhere drooling in their food.

Edward shook his head not in disgust but in a small amount of pity for the people he had known so well. Every day he would see someone in the obituaries he had known for years. After a while you regretted picking up the paper anymore. He was tired of being treated like he was already dead by the younger people who spoke with him. It was very sad knowing he would soon be just another forgotten memory like his friends and family before him.

Edward always enjoyed eating here. The reason was unclear to him, but today everything he ate or drank seemed tasteless. He tried to shake off any ill thoughts of those around him and to see them for what they were. This did not serve him well. Without a word, he placed his money on the table and walked from the coffee shop and down the street. There was another matter he was awaiting that should come to a close by the time he arrived at home. This was the one thing he most wanted to happen above all else.

Edward walked slowly down the gravel road and arrived at his home two hours before Betty would have his supper ready. Easing through the back door, he evaded Betty until he could get to the living room. He could see her standing by the kitchen window and looking out, hoping to see him coming home. It wasn't the time to talk to her, not until he could make his call.

Carefully he dialed a number he had buried deep within his memory. After the second ring, a gruff voice answered. "This is Doug, what can I do for ya?"

Edward laughed low, "Doug, this is Edward. Were you able to get that number for me?"

Papers rattling in the background sounded reassuring to Edward. "Got the number right here. Be careful, Edward, and if you need help, call me."

Taking the number, Edward wrote it on the palm of his hand. "Does anybody know you have this number?"

Doug grunted into the receiver. "Nobody knows but you and me. I prefer it stays that way."

Edward looked to see where Betty had gone to. Turning back to the phone, he almost whispered. "Thanks, it will stay with me. Don't worry about that. I have to get off the phone before Betty gets here. Check your mailbox tomorrow before the mailman gets there."

Before Doug could speak another word, the line went dead. Just after Edward placed the phone back into the cradle, Betty popped into the room. "Bein' sneaky, are ya?"

Edward just smiled and laid his head back against the chair cushion, closing his eyes. Betty was confused because he did not argue with her. Thinking he may be feeling tired, she left him to rest by the open window.

The next morning Betty had his breakfast piping hot and waiting for him. The smile on his face would have lifted the spirits of the dead.

"What's wrong with you? You're grinnin' like a goat eatin' briars," Betty said.

Edward wiped his mouth and leaned forward, holding his coffee cup in both hands. "Yesterday I made arrangements for that snake belonging to Lena to get what's comin' to him. I believe it is time for this upstart to get a taste of his own medicine."

Betty stood from the table, glaring at Edward with wide eyes. "Lord, Edward, what did you do? She has enough of a mess on her hands."

Edward placed the cup gently back on the table and winked at her. "You know yourself country boys have their own ways of getting to people who think they can do what they want."

"You can't have the man kilt for not makin' you happy. That's her concern, not yours," Betty squawked.

Edward lifted his hand to silence her. "Hear me out, Betty. The little girl is not a floor mat. People like him have a way of treating people around them with no respect. His health is not an issue. I can guarantee you not a hair on his head will be harmed. What *is* going to happen will not be known until after I'm dead and buried. I promise you won't miss a thing when the time comes."

Betty shook her head and started walking away, muttering to herself. "That crazy old man is gonna be the death of me yet."

Just as Betty rounded the pantry door, she heard a small knock on the back door. Peeping around the corner, she called out for Lena to enter.

Betty came from the pantry with her flowered apron filled with fresh vegetables. "You'll have to excuse me, I'm getting these ready for supper tonight."

Lena laughed lightly and helped Betty empty the apron onto the counter. Betty leaned in close and whispered, "That cranky old goat is up to somethin' again. See if he'll talk to ya, and let me know what it is. You really should get to know what makes him tick. It's true Celia was everything to him and more besides. I have something for you that will let you see that there is more to him than meets the eye.

"I found this letter when I was doing some cleaning around here. There is a poem he wrote to her on the day they were married. Never seen anything like it myself. Have to say it almost made me cry, the way he felt about her. Don't let him know you have this, or we all may be looking for a place to go to."

Reaching into her apron pocket, Betty pulled out a yellowed envelope and handed it to Lena. "Best read it fast 'fore he gets in here and catches us."

Lena pulled the yellowed pages from the envelope and began to read. The words came deep from Edward's heart and flowed on the paper with a purity she had never known. He had titled the poem "The Perfect Rose."

Along life's narrow and rocky roads,
I walked in search of the perfect rose.
Through gardens of stone and forest fair,
Yet none to be found, nor even compare.
Many were the days the search was in vain,
The essence of the rose, in my mind remained.
This perfect rose, you say, does not exist.
Your quest is in earnest, yet still you insist!
Petals of scarlet so rich with love,
A symbol of beauty for the gods above.
This vision of elegance for all time stands still,
A moment in her shadow is life fulfilled.
Oh sweet rose, I yearn for thee,
I long for your love to comfort me.
In the twilight of time my memories lie in sweet repose,
Your beauty is thine own, for how can one insult,
The perfect rose.

Lena stood speechless for a few seconds. "Betty, it is almost hard to believe he felt this strongly about her even on their wedding day."

Before she could finish speaking, Edward appeared at the door. The two of them were still head-to-head when Edward slipped through the door and grabbed his hat and a fresh apple from the bowl. "You two can butt heads all you want, but I am still not going to tell you my business. Not now or later, Betty." As Edward slipped past Betty, he slapped her behind firmly and walked out of the back door.

Betty jumped and squealed loudly. Her face reddened deeply, and it had rendered her almost speechless. Almost! "I told you the old fart had lost his mind."

The sound of Edward's laughter could be heard ringing through the kitchen. Lena, though slightly embarrassed for Betty, could not help but giggle as she opened the refrigerator door. "Don't worry, Betty, I won't tell on you."

Betty threw the dishcloth, barely missing Lena's head. "You can go out there with him. Sometimes I would swear you really are kin to him."

Lena stood in the doorway just off the porch. Sticking her head back through the door, she snickered. "The harmony here makes me want to sing."

Lena barely made it completely out the door before a tomato hit the door frame next to where her head previously had been. Betty called after her, "You tell that old goat he has a big mouth, and you are just as bad as he is."

Edward watched as Lena walked briskly across the yard to the bank of the river. She was still laughing when she reached his side.

"What do you find so funny, young lady?" he asked.

Lena finally was able to contain her laughter. "Betty said to tell the old goat he has a big mouth, and I am more than likely kin to you in every way."

Edward looked down at his shoes and grinned. "Now you are getting on her good side."

Lena looked at Edward. "Guilty as charged, your honor. I plead for mercy from the court. Ice cream would be better, but I'll settle for forgiveness."

Edward smiled lightly. "You are forgiven—just make sure it happens again so she doesn't think you don't like her anymore."

Lena nodded and held her silence for a moment.

Edward caught her reaction very quickly. "I see she had something else to say. Would you like to share?"

A look of longing came into her eyes while she spoke softly, very intent on letting Edward know how she felt. "Betty said we were probably related. I take that as a compliment, Edward. If you and Celia had been my parents, I expect life would have turned out very different for me. You can adopt me if you want. On my end, you are too late—I have already adopted you."

Edward was taken aback. He had no idea Lena felt that way about him and Celia. It lifted his heart greater than any gift ever given to him. Words did not want to form on his lips. For what seemed to be an eternity, he could not find the words, no matter how he tried. He looked deep into her eyes and found she was telling the truth, straight from her heart.

Lena tried to counter for him in an awkward moment. "Don't just do something, stand there!"

Edward shook his head, laughing hard as he sat down in his chair. "For once that old bat was right. You really are as bad as I am. Welcome to the family, and bring your own medication. Don't forget, Brad will be here tonight, so wear your best brogans."

Lena reached into her pocket and pulled out a handful of Betty's molasses cookies. "Have a cookie and hush."

Edward grabbed her tiny hand just as she was about to bite into the cookie. "You can't eat that. You are taking your life in your hands. Once you start, they become a habit you can't break."

Lena looked down at the cookie questioningly. "I thought you liked these, so I stole a few for you."

Lena finished off two of the cookies before taking another breath. "How about Celia's molasses cookies, were they good?"

Edward turned his head away for a second, and then back to look into her eyes. "My Celia could make a molasses cookie that would make you cry. They were horrible, to say the least. I never had the heart to tell her. I would take the cookies with me when I walked through the woods and throw them away when she wasn't looking. The bears didn't want them either.

"One afternoon she nearly caught me in the act, so I had to eat the cookies. All I have to say is, thank God for whiskey!"

"You have no shame, Edward." Lena bit into the cookie and looked at him with tears of laughter in her eyes. "Does this mean I get to eat your share of Betty's cookies?"

Edward pulled his hat down low over his brow and lighted his pipe. "Not a chance."

Chapter Fourteen

Edward rose from his bed the next morning and dressed quickly. Grabbing his hat and cane, he made his way down the path and headed for town. He walked slowly in the beginning until he reached an unmarked mailbox belonging to Doug. Looking about him, he reached into his pocket and withdrew an envelope. The door of the mailbox squeaked loudly, and he slid the envelope in. He assured himself the door was closed tightly and returned the same way he had entered the street.

Betty never asked where he had been after he returned home. Her mind seemed to be occupied elsewhere. Edward knew Doug would make the arrangements he had asked. The other arrangements were left strictly up to him.

Edward sat and read the daily paper until Betty left the house to go and buy groceries. From his window, he watched her until she was out of sight and he was assured she would not be back. Picking up the phone next to his chair, he carefully dialed the number Doug had given him earlier. A female voice on the other end of the line answered sweetly. "Hello."

Edward leaned in closer, lowering his voice. "I believe you were expecting my call."

"One moment, please," she said.

In the next instant a man with a soft mountain accent answered. "How can I help you?"

"I would like for someone to taste his own medicine," Edward said.

"What would you like done and for how long?" Edward could hear each breath the man took as he talked.

"I believe six months should take care of it. His vanity needs to be addressed, as well as his luck."

The man on the other end of the line coughed heavily. "I need a name and anything you can give me for this to work."

Edward filled him in on everything he wanted to know. "Can you tell me when this will start taking effect?"

The man coughed again loudly. "Things go right, your man will start changing as of tomorrow. It will be subtle in the beginning, and then get worse. At the end of six months, he will be good as new again in most ways."

Edward snickered. "He has a touch of tomcat in him, will that be affected also?" he asked pensively.

The voice came back on the line. "That will not be a problem. In fact, I will throw that in for free."

"Thank you very much. Should you need something extra, your contact will call me and you will have it." As quickly as Edward finished speaking, he heard the line on the other end click heavily.

Edward was satisfied with his decision. He had contacted a witch to do his bidding, instead of doing something that would have him thrown in jail. At his age, jail time was out of the question.

Satisfied, he grabbed his hat and cane as he hurried out of the house.

Lena opened the curtains to her mountain retreat to let the sunshine enter her life. It was good to feel the breath of life warming her face. Just as she turned away from the window, a soft knock on the front door drew her attention. She walked softly across the living room and bent to peer through the peephole located in the front door.

She saw a man standing there whom she did not know and was afraid to let him in. She called out to him: "Who is calling, please?"

The man smiled nicely and introduced himself as an associate of her old friend.

Lena unlocked the door carefully and allowed him inside. "I am here to attend to your roach problem," he said bluntly as he handed her his business card.

She nodded and handed the card back to him. "I thought I saw some of them in the kitchen and bedroom. You may want to check there first."

The gentleman smiled and began to unpack several pieces of sophisticated electronic equipment. Without a word, he started to scan each room, trying to find anything used for surveillance purposes. Lena followed him from room to room, always referring to the listening devices as roaches. The gentleman reached her bedroom and discovered a tiny bug placed in her phone. He pulled it deftly from the phone and placed it in a small metal box.

There were a total of nine listening devices found throughout the house. Some had been there as long as a year. Leaving them all on a table, he motioned to Lena to be very quiet until he told her to speak.

"I could not find any roaches in your home. I sprayed it thoroughly just to be safe. If any should return after this, we will take care of them for you. Your account is in good standing with us, and this visit falls under your contract for yearly pest control."

The gentleman winked at her as he handed her a note. *This will take care of everything for now. If you suspect anything, call us and I will be here. Now you need to thank me loudly and clearly while I leave in case I missed something. Charles has a scrambler on his phone, so calls to or from him are never understandable to an outside party.*

Lena looked at him with deep gratitude. "Thank you very much for coming."

The man closed the box containing the nine listening devices and walked casually from the house. Lena breathed a sigh of relief. Charles had not let her down. It was hard to accept the fact everything she said and did was going on a tape recorder somewhere for her husband to hear. She had done nothing wrong. Gerald should know this, especially by now. The guilty are always paranoid about something. Deep within her mind, she began to wonder what he was doing now.

The next two days came and went as though time had grown wings and gained flight. Edward had told her he needed to go out of town on some business and would not be back until Sunday. They agreed for Lena to come to the house on Sunday to have dinner with them. Betty had promised her baby back ribs with her secret hot sauce. She said it would tempt the devil himself for another bite.

Lena traveled back to her home in Richmond, hoping she would start some fireworks when her husband came home. Lena stepped through the front door and was greeted immediately by her housekeeper, Gena. "I am so glad you are home, Mrs. Leicester. Maybe some kind of sanity can come from it."

Lena grabbed her gently by the arms and looked at her. "Has something happened?"

Gena shook her head. "If you had not come home today, I would have quit tomorrow. Mr. Leicester doesn't care what he says or does any longer."

Lena smiled evenly. "I am asking you not to quit. Things are going to change very soon. Trust me, you won't be sorry."

Gena nodded and reached for Lena's bags. She picked them up and headed for the stairs. Gena then stopped at the foot of the stairs and called out to her: "Welcome home, Mrs. Leicester."

Lena laughed easily and walked through the house to the kitchen. She reached for the first thing she found cold to drink and poured a tall glass of it. Taking her glass from the countertop, she kicked off her shoes and walked barefoot out of the back double doors and found a seat on the patio. It was a pleasant place to be. The summer sun made the water of the swimming pool glitter like diamonds. Closing her eyes, she tried to relax as much as possible. The thought of Gerald being home at any time was not an entertaining idea.

Opening her eyes slowly, she looked about her. Everywhere she looked was a reminder of the ever-increasing greed of her husband. Everything was new—there was nothing by the pool or in the landscaping that had not been changed. It was obvious it was designed to impress visitors.

Lena reached beside of her lounge chair and picked up the phone. Punching in the correct code, she started retrieving the old messages that had not been erased from its history. The majority of the messages involved business deals, while others were very suggestive for evening activities. These messages left no name attached to them. Smiling sardonically, she pressed the button and erased all of the messages, including the current ones. Eventually this would cause quite a stir in Gerald's social life. *Gena is right, Gerald, you are getting a little too bold!*

By the end of the day, Lena had visited every room in the house with the intention of finding some little something that may help her exact her revenge upon him. Gena spotted her as she was leaving the master bedroom. "Is there anything I can help you do, Mrs. Leicester?" she asked.

Lena stopped and leaned heavily against the wall next to the bedroom door. "Yes, you can. I noticed there is still a strong smell of someone else's perfume. Do you know who she is?"

Gena's face slightly colored from embarrassment. "Yes, it belongs to Miss Shepard. She has been your husband's latest trophy. If I may be honest here, I stopped covering the perfumes after he threatened me with dismissal if I said anything. He also said he would see to it I was never hired for any other household in Richmond."

Lena's eyes blazed. "You don't have to worry about any of that. You work for me, not him. I will make sure you are taken care of. When is he due to be home today?"

Gena held a look of silent relief on her face. "He said he would be home by seven at the very latest because he was expecting you to be here."

Lena smiled and grabbed her by the hand. "Very good. I say you and I can go downstairs and fix some dinner for the two of us. That way we can have a chance to talk about what goes on here. When he gets home, he can fend for himself. You don't have to worry; I will take care of things from there. One other thing, if you please. I would like for you to remove the lingerie belonging to the young lady and place it on his desk. I will write the note for you to place on top of it."

Gena smiled and agreed as she watched Lena proceed back downstairs out of sight.

A plan was starting to form deep within Lena that brought a smile of satisfaction to her face. Her purpose was to lead Gerald to think she would dismiss his affairs and all would be better between them. The lull before the storm would be one to make even the Greek gods jealous of her. If all went well, Gerald would be the one doing the crawling for a change.

Lena was not aware what Edward had arranged for him. If she had known, there would have been a difference in her plans.

At the stroke of seven on the clock Gerald opened the front door and strolled easily to the kitchen. Gena quickly excused herself and left the house for the evening. Gerald smiled as though all was well in the world. Leaning over Lena, he kissed her gently and told her he was glad she was home. It was repulsive to have him anywhere near her, but she played her part with the ease of an Oscar-winning actress.

Gerald sat across from her, holding both her hands in his own. She knew he had already been in his office and had read the note she left attached to the lingerie. As he talked, he used all of his old methods of trying to smooth things over when he had been caught doing what he did best: conning the world and those who placed trust in him.

Feeling his message had come through to her and she was convinced the fault lay with her and was hers alone, he continued on. He wanted them to continue their lives and forget what had happened to bring distrust into their lives.

"Yes, I suppose we can carry on as though nothing has ever happened, can't we?" she lied.

Gerald sat next to her and pulled her closer to him. It was difficult to let him touch her in any way.

"I want you to know I didn't want any of this to happen." His lie was blatant. "I want things between us to be the same as they were before. I am sorry if I hurt you. It will never happen again, I swear it. You have to think, I needed you and you were not here. That is why I filled that space with someone whom I care nothing about."

Lena leaned closer. "Was she the only woman you took to my bed?"

Gerald looked straight into her eyes and lied to her once more. "I never had but the one affair, and it lasted for a very short time. Can you forgive me? Can we start over?" Gerald knew he must convince her for the simple fact he didn't know exactly what she was trying to do to him. It was in the interest of self-preservation and nothing more.

It was everything Lena could do to keep from strangling him for the blatant lies. "I will forgive you this time. However, I need some space to work things out. I will be returning to the mountains tomorrow. I am going back to the cabin, and you can come when you have the time."

Gerald was adamant in his thoughts that Lena knew close to nothing of his activities. He did not worry Gena may have said anything to Lena, for she was afraid of losing her livelihood. He rose from his chair like a king from his throne. It was obvious to Lena there was not a humble bone in his body.

"Gerald, before you go, you need to know I will be taking Gena to the cabin with me when I leave here," she said with a smile.

There was an urge to tell Lena it wasn't going to happen. Gerald just nodded his head in agreement and walked away. He thought this may be to his benefit because Gena could no longer witness his actions. In his mind, housekeepers were a dime a dozen.

Shortly after Gerald left the room, Lena made a call to Gena's home and informed her of her plans. The joy of this news could be heard easily over the phone.

Chapter Fifteen

Edward stood on the bridge by Angel Falls watching as the clear waters cascaded down the mountainside and flowed smoothly over the rocks. Life was strange even at the best of times. Miracles appeared when you need them most. He had seen everything he had ever wanted to see in his time, although he had wondered about many places. This was his home, his refuge from the world outside of his door.

He leaned on the rail of the bridge, smoking his pipe and thinking of the time that was left to him. Was it years, hours, or even possibly minutes? He had few regrets, and the precious memories of all that he had ever known flooded his thoughts at that instant.

His memory about small things in his everyday life was starting to fade. His inability to recall the simple things irritated him to no end. The strongest memories were of Celia. This brought little comfort knowing that sometimes he confused what had really happened, realizing later what the truth was. Was this what others called senility? If this was the case, he would rather become mute and let life come to its end.

As of late he began to notice his body trembled when he tried to associate himself with a small task. Edward had never worn glasses in his life, but now his vision was, at best, becoming a haze-covered world of the old. It was not a cataract, but his vanity refused to wear simple reading glasses to make life easier.

The sound of the rushing waters brought him back to his feet planted firmly on the bridge. He didn't know where he was or how he had gotten there. It frightened him. He looked around and nothing was familiar. Losing control, he felt tears of desperation come to his eyes. It was not unlike a small child lost in a crowd and unable to find his mother.

The words rushed from his throat in a strangled plea for help. "Celia, help me. Oh, please help me!"

Celia's voice came to him as if she stood by his side. "I am here, Edward. Follow my voice, and I will take you home safely."

Edward obeyed every word his precious Celia spoke to him. She guided him back onto the path and stayed with him until he reached the edge of his yard beyond the woods. As her voice faded from his ears, Edward looked around, wanting to thank her for saving him. She was neither heard nor felt.

Betty nearly ran across the yard when she spotted Edward emerging from the woods. He was visibly weak and had difficulty walking a steady stride. "Mr. Edward, you have been gone a long time. I was coming to look for you when I seen you come out the woods. Let me get you in the house so you can rest a spell."

Edward did not fight or resist her desire to get him inside of the house. The look on Betty's face told him a great deal. He had frightened her, unintentionally, but frightened her all the same. It was ironic to him that he had also badly frightened himself.

Betty noticed his hat and his cane were missing. From the direction he had come from, she suspected they were still somewhere close to the falls. She would have to go and get them after she was sure of his safety.

Betty sat Edward in his favorite chair by the window and placed a soft pillow behind his head. He barely moved as she attended to what she felt he needed. "Mr. Edward, you stay here while I go and find your hat and cane. I will be back fast as I can."

Edward nodded his agreement and closed his eyes. The only thing he wanted now was to forget what had happened to him.

Betty glanced behind her once more to assure herself that Edward was not in any danger. She kept her straw hat on a hook close by the back door. Quickly she passed through the living room and walked into the kitchen. She thought she had heard an odd sound just before she entered through the kitchen door. It was just enough to catch her attention, but almost unnoticeable in the beginning. Looking toward the back door where her straw hat was neatly hung, she saw Edward's hat on the hook next to her own. His cane was still swaying as if it had just been placed there.

"My word!" she exclaimed. Betty knew for a fact Edward had left the house with his hat and cane because she had given them to him as he stood on the porch. She watched him walk away from the house with both of the items in plain sight! The hat and the cane could not have belonged to anyone except Edward. They were both a fixture in his world.

Without hesitation, Betty spoke to the air about her. "Miss Celia, if you done this, I thank you for it. My old bones won't ready for a trip to the falls today."

Betty still stood looking around her in hope of catching some small glimpse of the person responsible for returning Edward's belongings. Without another word, she slipped from the kitchen silently and returned to sit by Edward.

He slept restlessly through the rest of the evening. Betty did not try to wake him for his supper. She waited diligently for him to awake on his own. When he was awake, she would fix his dinner for him as she always had.

Living with Edward had been much easier than he ever thought it was for her. She had no doubt that if she was in trouble or just needed a friend, he was always there. The teasing only added a little spice to life. The time was coming when she would lose Edward as she did her husband. She dreaded the day almost worse than any other. It would be a time of loss like no other. They had been companions for a very long time. Edward was family to her above all else.

Edward awakened to the dampness of nightfall caressing his cheek. Opening his eyes, he saw Betty sitting across from him reading a book.

She looked up and grinned. "Let me know when you want your dinner, and I'll get it ready for you."

Edward nodded slowly and rose shakily from his chair. "I think I will step out on the porch and smoke for a little while. You rest yourself, and I'll let you know when I am ready."

Betty just nodded and let him have some time for himself without argument. He needed to eat to keep up his strength, but there are times when someone you love is not to be pushed into what is best for them. From the window she could see him sitting in his rocking chair. Knowing he was close by and having nothing to worry about, she returned to her reading.

Edward stared across the yard and toward the rolling waters of the river. The events of the day had drained him miserably. He convinced himself this wouldn't happen again. Lifting his chin in defiance of life, he laughed softly.

The stars were beginning to show against the dark blue sky over him. Absently, he tried remembering each of the constellations he had learned as a child. Each and every one of them came to his mind easily.

Edward loved the stars and the simple pleasures they brought to him. They were things of beauty in the night for all to see. Time had a way of letting you know the most brilliant works of man have passed you by without so much as a second thought. You get caught up in life's moments concerning your little corner and very little else. In his lifetime, man had journeyed to the moon. A microwave oven had taken the place of people really knowing how to cook at home, and the economy dictated both parents needed jobs to ever obtain any of the small things they wanted to enjoy life. Children found it more convenient to stay inside and play with their computers and other electronic toys rather than gain the knowledge and the wonders of the world around them. Children saw bears in the zoo instead of seeing them in their natural habitat. How many children these days would survive if the electricity went away, along with their way of life?

Survival of the fittest. These children today would be the last to even have the knowledge of how to obtain food from sources other than a can. Both times were good in their own way. Couple the old world with the new. If the two worlds were combined as they should be, the world may be a better place for all. What have the wars he had lived through accomplished? It was obvious very little had come from them other than a lot of families on both sides losing the things they held so close to them. These are things that can never be replaced. The turn of the century was just around the corner, and the world was still in need of a good bowel movement to get rid of the idiots. Communism, socialism, and a host of things listing man's inhumanity to his fellow man were still among us. The irony of it all was our leaders say we have won.

Edward stopped in his tracks. Rambling through times already gone was never going to solve anything. The key was to enjoy what he had left to him. He held no great power to ease the woes of the world, and he was old enough that the responsibility of it all would have to be left to others. Sometimes this was much harder than trying to get an alligator in a suitcase.

Reaching into the pocket of his shirt, he pulled out his pipe. He sat looking at it for a few seconds, thinking about all the years he had enjoyed smoking it. Shrugging his shoulders, he struck a match to the tobacco and watched the smoke curling from the bowl. *Closest thing to heaven I have ever seen!*

The next morning, with the rising of the sun, Edward came to sit on the porch again. After about an hour, Edward rose from his chair and descended the steps with ease. Strange how the weakness of his limbs only came at the most inconvenient times. The grass beneath his feet felt as soft as a cloud. Looking down, he realized he had forgotten to put his shoes on. No matter, it did a body good to feel the earth beneath its feet now and again.

Edward walked a few yards to a nearby rosebush and bent to catch the aroma of its flowers in bloom. These were American Beauty roses. The plant came from his sister's last visit to his home. Holding one of the blooms gently in his hand, he thought of how beautiful it was. It still amazed him how the beauty of the world always shone through when times were at their ugliest.

The sound of a car coming up the gravel path brought Edward back from his thoughts. The girl behind the wheel smiled and waved as she pulled into his driveway. On the side of the car, he saw the sign announcing a local exterminator. The young lady crawled from her car and approached him with a pleasant smile and a big hello.

"Yes, and hello to you. What can I do for you today?" Edward asked.

The young lady handed him her business card and continued much as if he had said nothing at all. "You have a lovely home, sir. I am here to see if I can help you keep your home free from pests. Are you having trouble with roaches?"

Edward looked into her eyes and smiled. "I appreciate you being so thoughtful. I just moved back in a little while ago and have kept an eye out for pests. Haven't seen any pests yet, and I can honestly say my roaches are very satisfied. Not so much as a grumble from any of them. It's my best guess they are very happy here."

The young lady had no idea what to say from that point. With a quick thank-you, she hurried back to her car and left Edward standing and staring after her.

Betty stepped out onto the porch and put her hands on her hips. "I heard that, you old coot! She was trying to help you out a little bit. I don't think she was very amused with your crap."

Edward stared at Betty, a look of feigned shock covering his face. "I just answered the lady's question as best I knew how. What is wrong with that?"

Betty could not keep a straight face any longer. "I have to admit, that was funny. Come on in and get your breakfast before your happy roaches get to it."

Betty smiled sweetly as Edward sat down at his plate and began to eat. Looking up from his plate, he saw her smiling at him. "You must have slept well last night. You seem to be mighty happy this morning."

"Yes, I did sleep well. I had an idea for you and me today. Why don't we go down to Cliff's Diner and get supper tonight? It's my treat."

Edward laughed easily. "We can do that. Do I have to dress up or anything?"

"Nope, just come just like you are."

"I almost forgot—it's fish night at the diner. You haven't had any for a while. I'd be glad to go with you. There is a new movie playing down the street from the diner. What do you say we stop in and watch it? You get dinner, and I'll get the movie."

"That's a deal if I ever heard one. One more little thing I need to remind you about. You can have the popcorn, but not the chocolate-covered peanuts."

Edward nodded and thought, *We'll see what I can have and what I can't!*

Dinner was a disappointment to say the least. The fish was overcooked and nothing had the flavor it should have had, considering the boasting they did to promote it on the menu. The rest of the evening was much better, with a movie a man could sink his teeth into. Just enough action to get your heart pumping with a desire to see what was going to happen next.

Edward made his excuses to go to the restroom twice during the movie. An old man's bladder was fragile, you know. He slipped to the concession stand and bought two boxes each of Raisinets and Goobers. He believed he could slip by Betty and eat them when he returned home. There were a lot of places he could go and have his treats without her knowing.

Edward returned to his seat, secure in thinking his secret was safe. Betty sidled up to Edward's side and lowered her voice. "Before we get home, I want you to give me the peanuts and the raisins. If you eat them, you will get sick, and you know it!"

Edward drew back in shock. "What makes you think I have anything like that?"

Betty smirked. "You have chocolate on your breath already. I think you planned this out before you got here."

Edward reached into his pocket and handed her a box of each. She took them and placed the boxes in her purse. Reaching her hand out, she wiggled her fingers. "Now give me the rest of them. I know because you ate some of them and the boxes rattled when you sat down."

Grudgingly he handed them over and turned back to the movie.

Chapter Sixteen

Gerald felt a sense of relief when he returned home to find Lena had already left for the mountains. There had to be a change. He had not been as discreet as he should have been. All of this was on the verge of costing him a life of luxury. He was sure she believed every word he had said based on her actions. It was easier than he had suspected it would be.

Smiling, he headed upstairs and jumped into the shower. He felt dirty. Strange, he had never felt that way before. There was something he could not pinpoint, a certain odor in the air about him. It reminded him of a child's soiled diaper. He washed quickly and thoroughly, trying to rid himself of the offending odor.

Stepping from the shower, he toweled himself off briskly and threw the towel onto the floor. He had forgotten there was no longer anyone to pick up things behind him. He picked out his best suit and tie because he was planning to attend a nice new restaurant in the city with a young lady he had met in Dallas a few weeks ago. She had agreed to come and visit Richmond, and he would show her the sights. The odor was beginning to rear its ugly head once more, and he was unable to find its source.

While applying a quick dash of his best cologne, he heard a knock on the door that assured him his limousine had arrived on time and he would not be late. The chauffeur held the door for him as he climbed inside. The chauffeur closed the door quickly and climbed into the front, starting the engine. Gerald noticed he immediately closed the window between them. Inside of the limousine the odor was almost unbearable! He looked everywhere and could not find a reason for it.

Reaching the destination, the driver opened Gerald's door and stepped away from the car. The look on his face told Gerald that he appeared to smell the awful scent. Disregarding the odor as imagination, Gerald walked into the hotel lobby and straight for the elevators. Those who were standing in line and waiting for the lift drew back from Gerald and began to disperse, making excuses for not getting on the elevator.

Gerald paid little attention to them and walked through the open doors. As they closed behind him, the scent grew stronger again. It was difficult to be within the confines of the elevator walls.

Reaching the ninth floor, the doors opened and Gerald stepped out into the hallway, thankful for a breath of fresh air. He stopped, sniffing the air about him. The scent was gone. It seemed to have vanished when he stepped from the elevator.

His footsteps were hushed by the plush carpeting as he walked the hall looking for room 914. Once there, he straightened his tie and brushed a few hairs from his jacket. He knocked lightly on the door. The door opened and a very pretty young lady stood before him, her smile a thing of beauty.

Suddenly her face turned ugly, and she backed away from him, almost knocking over a lamp by the door. Gerald stayed where he was standing in the door. "What happened? What's wrong? Is anything wrong?"

She screeched at him. "For Pete's sake, do you always come to see a girl smelling like you just crapped your pants? Get the hell out! Just go away, and don't think you are going to call me again either!"

Gerald stood silently as the door slammed in his face. He did not smell anything other than the usual things they used to clean the rooms in these places. Everywhere he went inside the hotel, people avoided him. To avoid any more embarrassment, he exited the hotel as quickly as possible. The limousine he had rented for the night had left without him.

Finally, the third taxi he called was willing to take him home, but at double the price. Each had complained of the odor about him, and still he could smell nothing but the city around him.

The days passed quickly, and Gerald noticed whenever he began to try to get involved with a beautiful woman the strange scent would return. It did not take very long for Gerald to begin being very careful about anything he said to others.

How could this be happening to him? In the beginning he felt as though he were having some kind of breakdown. He still wasn't sure. Maybe the women were backing away from him because they felt he was too aggressive. Until he could get everything figured out, he felt he would just lie back and try to gain control again.

Gerald began to eat salads for lunch. Though he worked hard at the gym trying to stay fit to entice the ladies, he began to grow a bit of a bulge at his belt line. It did not matter what he ate or how he tried to control his diet, his stomach became more pronounced.

Sitting at his desk, Gerald's thoughts were not on his work. *I need to regain my control here. Lena has spent too much time in Hicksville. I think there has to be something there other than what my guys have told me. They insist she hasn't done anything I need to know about, but I'm not so sure. If I can find that certain little something, I can get her back where she belongs. This guy Edward must have a lot of money to be able to keep her coming back. She probably caught on to my guys and paid them to back me off. It's time I checked into this guy for myself.*

Like they say, when you need something done right, do it yourself. I believe the tapes they sent me have been edited for whatever reason, and I can't understand why they can't catch her on video. They told me she was always surrounded by other people or in a position that caused the film not to be any good. That's a lie! Anybody can be followed!

I am going to pack my bags and head for those mountains. I'll get the lowdown on this Edward guy and have her back under my thumb in no time.

Gerald spent the balance of the day making arrangements to be out of town for at least a week. He knew there would be questions, so he contrived a story that would cover his tracks until he could return to the office. He was due for a vacation and used this excuse to let people know he may not be available sometimes. He promised he would call the office as often as possible to make sure things were running smoothly.

Covering his tracks was important to him. He didn't want Lena or Edward to know he would be close by. Trying to ensure nobody would know where he was, he rented a car in Richmond and had his personal car dropped off in a storage area, where it would be waiting for his return. He couldn't help but laugh. They wouldn't suspect a thing and he would be able to find out for himself what the real situation was.

Once on the highway, he headed south on the interstate, humming a song he couldn't seem to get out of his head. The miles clicked by, and the only time he stopped was to refuel. He wanted to get to Asheville as soon as possible.

Some habits die hard, and with Gerald an ordinary hotel was out of the question. Nothing would do but the very best, regardless of the price!

He settled himself in Asheville's finest hotel and gathered his maps close to him. The information he had received placed Edward's house an hour and forty-three minutes from his location. Gerald brought his best camera along with a set of Zeiss binoculars to spy on his wife and her friend. He wanted to use the guise of a photographer. In those mountains, people by the hundreds came to take pictures. He would just be another to fill in the gap.

By the end of the first day, he was prepared for anything that confronted him.

Gerald slept like an angel that night and rose with the sun just peeking over the tops of the mountains. It was a glorious sight, but he knew he didn't want to waste time staring at it. He ate his breakfast hurriedly and grabbed a cup of coffee to take with him. The waitress stood a short distance from his table as she asked if there would be anything else for him. Gerald thanked her and wondered why she scurried from his table so quickly. The doors to the kitchen lay open just enough that he could see her talking with one of the other waitresses.

As was his habit, he stopped by the hostess standing at the door to thank her for the excellent service. She smiled prettily and asked if he had enjoyed his meal. His words were barely past his lips when she reeled back away from him, bearing a look bordering on sudden illness. "Sir, might I offer you some of our mints for the day?"

Gerald was insulted. He had never had bad breath in his life. That was one issue he could not afford with his social life. "I beg your pardon?"

The young lady looked as though she was about to retch. She covered her mouth and nose while she shoved the dish of mints toward him. In an instant she had disappeared from her podium, leaving Gerald where he stood.

Gerald shook his head in wonderment. He then strolled from the hotel to his rental car. Once inside, he breathed heavily into his palm and could detect no odor. The young lady must have been feeling ill and didn't realize it was not he who had a problem.

The engine started and idled smoothly as he reached for his seat belt. Pulling it across him, he realized he had gained another inch across his midsection. Cursing under his breath, he clicked the belt into place and threw the car into gear.

Gerald had little trouble finding an area in close proximity of Edward's home. Studying his topographical map, he discovered being able to have himself close enough to watch what was going on at the house was a different matter. He was determined not to be stopped, regardless of the terrain he had to cross.

Gathering his things, he made an attempt through the heavily wooded mountains. It was the third attempt since he had arrived in the area. The going was made difficult each time he reached an area called Wolf Creek. The creek had been swollen with water from the heavy rains prior to his trek into the mountains, leaving no way to cross. He was lucky today with the water table dropping just low enough for him to find passage to the other bank. Slipping on the rocks and the mud, he finally reached a path used by animals that he discovered. The heat of the day nearly brought him to his knees on more than one occasion before he realized he had reached Angel Falls and found relief.

He sat close by the falls and studied his map once more, sure he was near his destination. Mosquitoes buzzed around him, driving him into a frenzy of swatting them and wishing he had more than two arms to fight them with. His face felt swollen and tight from the bites he had endured.

Another hour and darkness would be upon him. Just beyond the falls, he walked across the wooden bridge, still never knowing he was already on the property belonging to Edward Caulfield. Within an hour, he saw the break in the trees ahead of him. He approached it slowly and stayed close by the trees.

From this point he could see the house clearly. Sitting back on his haunches, he could see the old oak by the river and two people sitting and talking to each other. He recognized Lena right away and drew in a sharp breath. She turned her head, looking in his direction. Gerald prayed she did not see him watching them. She returned to talking with an old man in a hat that had to be from the 1940s. Gerald refused to believe this man could be Caulfield. It had to be his father or an uncle. Gerald did not know the true age of Edward, although his investigators had told him. There were many things Gerald had grown to disbelieve through his paranoia. It felt strange to see her laughing and talking with great animation to this man.

As darkness approached, he watched her walk to her car and leave the old man and another woman as they waved good-bye to her.

It was going to be a long night. Gerald had brought some food with him in a small pack, but he did not know how long it would last. The distance from his car to the Caulfield house was time he had not figured into his plans. He would just have to wait.

Gerald watched the house diligently until nine o'clock, and then suddenly all the lights were turned off in the house. Did people here in Hicksville really go to bed with the chickens? This was a normal hour for going to bed for Caulfield. Gerald just had no idea what life here was like.

The stars above him appeared clean and clear in the night sky. He made a bed of leaves and lay down for the night. Before he realized it, he was already sleeping heavily.

The morning sun rose in the sky, greeting a new day. Gerald rolled over and tried to get up. Every bone in his body ached horribly. The bed of leaves could have never compared with the mattress adorning his bed. The aroma of fresh-brewed coffee accompanied by the delicious smell of bacon assaulted his senses. His mouth watered for even the slightest taste of the food being prepared inside of the house.

Reaching inside of his small pack, he pulled out a packet of beef jerky and unwrapped it silently. Taking a large bite of it, he nearly spat the contents on the ground in front of him. He grimaced. *How do hunters eat this stuff? It has all the nutrition of a pound of lard. Almost tastes the same too!*

Hearing the front door of the house slam, he looked up to see a large woman and the old man descending the porch steps. Gerald could hear her words plainly as she told the old man it was grocery day and he had to go. It was good for him to get out of the house for a change. The old man did not say a word. He just climbed into the passenger's side of the car and pulled his hat down over his eyes. Gerald chuckled. *You would have to be deaf not to understand what the woman said.*

If their grocery day was anything like the ones he had experienced, they would be gone for no less than an hour. This was the perfect time for him to see what was in the house. Nothing tells more about a man than the inside of his house.

Gerald waited patiently until the car was out of sight. He gave them another ten minutes to ensure they had not forgotten anything. No sound came from the old house or anywhere on the grounds. He thought he was safe to venture forward and see what was inside. He would check the doors, and if they were locked, he knew he could always break a window to gain entry. The cops around this burg would take forever to even think about who might have done it.

Keeping his eyes peeled for anyone around, he walked across the lawn and up onto the porch. Gerald knocked on the door and waited, listening for movement within the house. Hearing no sound, he tried to open the door. It opened almost at his touch. Smiling, he walked into Edward's house, never bothering to wipe his feet. He called out, and the answer he received was the echo of his own words.

The sight before him was pleasantly surprising. He ran his soft hands across the hand-carved trim and gave a low whistle. He was amazed at the beauty of it. The whole house was almost a masterpiece of craftsmanship. Walking from room to room, he looked at every picture hoping to see a photograph of Edward. He found none. The furniture was not the latest, but he had to admit, it was once very expensive for its time. His emotions bordered on envy.

Finding nothing out of the ordinary, he walked boldly into the kitchen. On top of the stove on a small plate was the bacon left over from breakfast. Gerald reached out and grabbed it, walking through the rest of the house as he ate. His greasy fingers left prints everywhere.

Reaching the stairs, he stopped by a small table where Edward had left his mail and a ring of keys. There were also a few small porcelain figurines on the tabletop. Gerald was fond of good porcelain, and he picked up one of the figures to examine it more closely.

"You don't belong here!" a hollow voice whispered to him.

Gerald whirled in his tracks. He thought he had been discovered trespassing. "Hello, I am here to see Edward. Is he available?"

The voice came to him again. He could not find where it was coming from. "Get out of my house! You are not welcome here."

The voice gave Gerald a feeling unlike anything he had ever experienced. "Come here where I can see you. I wish to speak with you."

The voice was that of a woman and the answer to his call was frightening. Celia began to slowly materialize before him to his right. "Get out of my house! You are a thief and a liar. Leave here now while you are still able."

Gerald began to tremble at the sight before him. He turned and started to run back toward the dining room, looking for an escape. The voice screamed at him as a plate smashed heavily on the wall next to his head. Gerald raised his hands, trying to cover his face. He darted to his left and was hit in the forehead with a porcelain figure he had seen in the sewing room. With every turn from room to room, he was assaulted by glass and figurines of all sizes. Reaching the back door, he felt two small hands grab him from behind and then push mightily. He sailed through the air, crashing through the screen back door and out onto the porch.

The ghostly voice called after him. "You will pay for what you have done. I know who you are!"

Jumping to his feet, he could still see the figure as it followed him across the yard. Reaching the edge of the woods, he looked back over his shoulder. The ghostly figure was nowhere to be seen.

Gerald hurried down the path, backtracking through the hills, trying to get back to his car. Blood trickling down his forehead made its way into his eyes. He wiped furiously at it, quickening his pace. A slight whine escaped from his lips as he saw the apparition once more, standing at the foot of the bridge. Gerald raced back into the forest and tried to find another way up the mountain and away from the apparition that had attacked him. At every turn he saw her, confusing him on which direction he needed to go.

Running, as if for his life, he became lost in a very short time. Just after midnight he caught sight of the highway and made his way onto the shoulder of the road. Gerald hitched a ride with a man in a pickup truck headed for Asheville. Gerald was afraid to go back and try to find his car, for fear the ghost would be waiting for him there.

The driver of the truck eyed him cautiously. "What happened, did your car break down?"

Gerald lied easily. "No, I was taking some pictures in the mountains and lost my way. I got lucky and found the highway just before you came along."

"Yep, you are lucky. This time of night, catching a ride with anybody besides a deputy is a streak of luck. Where did you come from?"

"I was walking some trails in the gorge."

The driver looked at Gerald and shook his head. "Well, I believe that explains all the cuts and scratches you have. That is bear country through there. You are real lucky you didn't run into one."

The sun was just coming up when Gerald walked into the lobby of the hotel. Just as he pushed the button to bring the elevator, a young lady handed him a sealed envelope. Thanking her, he stuck the envelope into his pocket and stepped inside, barely giving the doors time to open.

It was a blessing to be back in his room again after what he had experienced. He washed all the cuts gently and let the water run over him in an attempt to wash away his memories. But the sight of the apparition chasing him through the house refused to leave his thoughts.

Closing his eyes, he began to wash his hair. He always felt much cleaner when his hair was freshly washed. Humming softly, he massaged his scalp, trying to rid himself of the mud and dirt he had collected in the mountains. Glancing down at his feet, he saw the water deepening in the tub. He reached down and rubbed his hand over the drain. A thick wad of hair came away in his hand. Quickly, he rinsed the soap from his hair and toweled himself dry. Stepping to the mirror, he discovered some of his hair had fallen out. It appeared to be just a little, and he dismissed it for the returning thoughts of the apparition appearing before him.

Gerald had small cuts covering his arms and face. He shook his head in disgust as he applied an antiseptic to each of the cuts. Several were sure to scar. "Geez, the crazy bitch tried to kill me. I could have sworn it was a ghost or something. I probably just panicked."

Walking back into the bedroom, he switched on the television and reached for the envelope the young lady had given him. The return address was from the car-rental company. Tearing open the envelope, he read the note quickly. In his anger he wadded the note into a ball and flung the paper across the room. "I can't believe this. The damned park service towed my car while I was wasting time with Caulfield."

Gerald reached over to pick up the phone with the intent of calling the rental company. The light on the phone was blinking, notifying him there was a message awaiting his attention. He dialed the number and was immediately connected to his message center. The voice of his secretary came on the line. He could not think of how she would know where he was—he had told no one where he would be.

"Gerald, I have bad news for you. Sorry for the call, but this is important. Western Coal and Steel has canceled their contract with us, and their attorney has notified us of their intention to sue. We have forty-eight hours to respond to the charges. Call as soon as possible so I know what to do."

Gerald swore violently and slammed the phone back into its cradle. He knew that was a twelve-million-dollar contract, and the loss of it would not be taken lightly by the board. As far as Western suing them, he was not worried. The corporation had a bank of lawyers that would tear Western apart in a court of law. The only thing he didn't want was Lena's father getting wind of the situation. Western had been with the old man almost from the beginning.

Pacing the floor, he tugged at his bottom lip and tried to think of what he must do. Picking up the phone, he called his office and told them he would be back in Richmond by the following morning.

Chapter Seventeen

Gerald was able to charter a small plane and return to Richmond almost immediately. He tried his best to reach his office in a timely manner, but it was not meant to be. Just after lunch he walked through the doors of his outer office and approached his secretary.

Glancing up from her work, she asked, "Yes, sir, how may I help you today?"

She did not recognize Gerald!

Gerald sneered, "Cut the crap and tell me what has happened before I meet with the board."

His secretary sat with a startled look upon her face. "Gerald, what happened to you? If you hadn't spoken to me, I would have not known it is you."

Gerald straightened, standing stiffly. "What do you mean by that?"

"Look at yourself. Your face is cut up. Your hair is seriously thin, and I have never seen you with your stomach hanging over your belt. I'm sorry, but you really need a shower too. What is going on?"

Gerald knew he had a few cuts, and he had showered and shaved before he came to the office. This lady behind the desk had been his lover many times over, and now she seemed repulsed by the sight of him.

Before he could bring himself to answer her, the phone on her desk buzzed. She answered with a voice bordering on animation. "Mr. Leicester's office. Yes, sir, I will inform him the moment he comes in. Thank you for calling."

She looked at Gerald. "Bad news, Gerald, they know you are in the building, and you have been ordered to the boardroom immediately."

Gerald laughed. "Ordered by whom? I run this company. Nobody orders me anywhere!"

"It would seem your wife's father has entered the picture on this one, Gerald. I would suggest you clean up a bit and get down there."

Gerald refused to believe he looked as horrific as his secretary had said. Glancing in the mirror as he walked by, he saw little of what she was describing of him. With a small wave of his hand, he walked away and down the hall to the boardroom. The heavy door swung open, and Gerald saw all the members of the board of directors already seated. In his chair at the head of the long table sat Lena's father. There appeared to be nowhere for him to sit for the meeting. Before he could speak, Lena's father began to address the board.

"At one fifteen Eastern time I was contacted by the lawyers representing Western Coal and Steel Corporation. As all of you know, Joseph Benning has been dealing with us since the conception of this company. That's over thirty-five years, gentlemen. His son was overseeing the company in his absence. He is trying to retire from the business.

"This fiasco has brought him back into the chair, and he is not happy to say the least! On the table you will find the notes informing you of everything involved here. I want answers, and I will have them today, or I can—and will—dissolve the entire business. You will all be out of a job.

"If this goes to court, our reputation as being the number-one steel supplier for the nation will be destroyed. I can assure you he has that power.

"Mr. Benning's company was in the process of building a one-hundred-story office complex for some very influential people. Let me emphasize this. They are connected in ways many of you would never understand.

"Our portion of the contract was only twelve million. We were to receive another contract if and when they were satisfied with our services. They are not satisfied gentlemen to say the least. It would seem they have been delivered an inferior-grade steel that has been poorly fabricated without any certificates of welding X-ray by the government inspectors who were supposed to be on the site. This is unacceptable."

Lena's father looked down at the table in deep thought, tapping the marble top with his pen. "Lives have been lost here. Fathers of children, husbands with hopes of a bright future. The first two floors collapsed beneath them as they were trying to make a living using our products. The repercussions from all of this are already circling the globe. Every news organization you can think of is having a field day trying to gut us before we can find the facts.

"The gentleman to my left is the legal representative for us. In all of my years I have never had to answer any charges amounting to the magnitude of what has been brought before us today.

"Mr. Cooper has assured me the families of the men who lost their lives will be compensated as best we can. That does not bring them home, but it's all we can do for the time being. The rest of you return to your duties and get me some answers for who is responsible. Mr. Leicester, I will see you in your office following this meeting."

Gerald swallowed hard and eased himself out through the double doors, following the other men. Passing them by, he made his way to his office as quickly as possible. He did not know what to expect or what Lena's father already knew about deals he had made along the way. It was a vicious game of cat and mouse.

It was too late to worry. He would just have to try to let him do all of the talking. Gerald heard the door of his office close and turned to see Lena's father standing just a few feet from him.

"My God, Gerald, what has happened to you? You look like a reject from a haunted house."

Gerald had no idea how to explain his appearance. "I haven't got a clue. I just started to gain weight suddenly. I have an appointment to see my physician this afternoon," he lied carefully.

Lena's father pulled a chair away from the desk and sat down. "I want you to get to the bottom of this no later than the end of today. I don't care about any appointments with customers other than what we have before us. This is very serious, Gerald. If the government steps in, my career and everybody around me is going down. Have you made any arrangements with anyone concerning the steel that was used?"

Gerald shook his head and Lena's father continued. "If you have, I need to know now, so hopefully we can cover our tracks. I don't think we will ever be able to recover from what the news media has already done to us. I depended on you to make sure nothing like this could ever happen, and you have let me down."

Gerald stood from behind the desk and leaned forward menacingly. "I had nothing to do with this, and I do not care for the implication that I could have been stupid enough as to sell inferior steel to one of your best friends, not to mention he is also one of our best accounts."

Lena's father stood from his chair, leaning forward with his hands on the desk. They were nearly nose-to-nose. His voice was barely above a whisper. "Listen to me very carefully, Gerald. Deals are made every day between large firms such as ours. The answers will come to me as they always do, and I will retaliate against *anybody* who stands between me and a fortune. I worked too hard to see it all disappear like dust in the wind.

"I don't give a damn who it is behind it, I just want his head! That is one thing I can assure you I will have. As far as your intelligence is concerned, I have always had doubts about it. You are here just because my wife wants you here and I have to live with her!"

Gerald swallowed hard and returned to his seat. Lena's father backed away from the desk and started for the door. "You have until the end of the day, Gerald." Reaching for the door handle, he spoke to Gerald over his shoulder. "And for the love of heaven, take a bath, Gerald. You smell like a sewer."

The door slammed behind Lena's father as he left the room. Gerald picked up the stapler from his desk and hurled it across the room. He was seething with anger. It was true he did not know for sure what had happened with the steel for Western. He had turned down the bid from Spain for a more lucrative offer from Africa. Domestic steel was out of the question with union prices being what they were these days.

Sweat poured from his body. He started making call after call, trying to figure out what had happened and when. The answers came to him in bits and pieces from his calls and the words of the other board members. Nothing was pointing to him, and he thanked all that was holy for that.

Late into the night, facts and figures were still pouring in concerning the steel for Western. Little by little, it was all coming together to complete a story Lena's father would have to be satisfied with.

Gerald pored over the information, praying he would never be found as being a party to a disaster that had made worldwide news. Turning on the television, he could hear nothing but the wails of newscasters denouncing his company. One of the broadcasters had also made reference to the possibility of the work of a terrorist. There was no end in sight of all the speculation flying through the air about him.

Just as he was reaching for the remote control, his desk phone buzzed, startling him. "Leicester here, can I help you?"

His secretary's voice came through loud and clear. "You have a call from the commerce ministry of Dubai on the secure line."

Gerald hastily reached for his other phone and leaned back in his chair. "Karina, how are you?"

"Save the patter, Gerald, this is not a social call," she said.

"I see, so how may I help you?"

"It is of great concern to many that you may want to release information concerning your business with us."

Gerald thought quickly. "I really do not see what our transactions have to do with anybody else. The bargain we made was confidential and was not to be submitted for any press releases."

Karina drew her breath in sharply. "There are times when people get into situations and try to save themselves at the expense of others. We have seen this happen many times."

"I can assure you everything is under control here. There has been no mention of any transactions between us and the people of Dubai."

"Gerald, it is a necessary thing that we must not be implicated in what has happened with your company. I hope you understand that."

"I understand fully, and you have no need to worry."

"This is good, because we have already delivered the documents proving to your board of directors that the steel you purchased was the finest to be found. Would you agree about the quality?"

Gerald noticed Karina's voice had taken on an almost threatening quality. "I wholly agree, and there was no problem with your products as we agreed on."

The phone line was silent. He realized she had already disconnected. Gerald knew he was covered from any liability. Karina had produced documentation to prove his innocence in the disaster. Now it was time to find fault with someone else. It was second- and third-grade quality, but nobody could prove it as long as the proper documentation was on file.

Gerald placed a call to Lena's father and assured him the documents releasing them from any liability were in.

Gerald returned home, exhausted from the day's events. It was a time when all was going wrong in his life and relief was nowhere to be found. Stripping his clothes off, he stepped onto the bathroom scales. He gasped as he saw he had gained nearly sixty pounds. Kicking the dirty towels out of his path, he headed for the shower.

The hot water rushing from the showerhead felt like heaven. He washed himself thoroughly and stepped out of the shower feeling rejuvenated. His hair was again coming off onto the towel when he dried himself. Looking into the mirror, he found it was coming out by the roots in patches.

He could not understand what was happening to him. Earlier in the day, Gerald had escaped the confines of his office to see his physician. The doctor had difficulty believing Gerald's story as to when all of his problems had begun. Nothing, in his experience, had ever taken place so rapidly. The doctor collected samples from Gerald to run some tests to find what had caused this sudden onset and the reason for the unsettling scent his body was emitting. He only advised him to back away from the table when he was full and cut out late-night eating habits. Gerald knew this was not the case, but his doctor just dismissed his words. Standing back in front of the mirror again, he grimaced. His body was a disgusting sight even to himself. Something had to be done to end his torment, and soon!

Chapter Eighteen

Lena had been a very busy woman since she had last seen her husband. His face, along with her father's company, had been all over the news. Things were moving too quickly for her, and she knew she had to make her plans before anything else could happen.

Gathering her courage, she called Charles for an update.

"This is Charles Messer, can I help you?"

"Charles, this is Lena, have you been listening to the news?"

"Yes, I certainly have. Which reminds me, we have a dossier on Gerald that makes you wonder why he wasn't in jail before now. I cannot believe the crap this guy has been doing. He wasn't alone in it, but he is the ringleader. Has he called you since you returned to the mountains?"

"No, but I was getting ready to call him or father."

"Don't call either of them for now, because the press is all over this and I want you clear of it. I fear his phone is probably tapped by now. There is little doubt the feds are already sniffing in his direction. I would like to talk to Edward Caulfield, if it's okay with you."

"Why do you want to talk to Edward? He knows nothing about any of this."

"I think Caulfield can be a great help in getting your revenge for you. From my sources, he knows a lot of people. You would be surprised."

"Okay, but take it easy on him. I don't want to worry him about any of this."

"Not to worry, he is on our side." Charles disconnected the call and returned to his paperwork.

Lena sat staring at the phone in her hand, wondering what Charles may talk to Edward about.

She decided to place another call, and she dialed Edward's number. Betty answered the phone on the first ring. Her voice was strained.

"Betty, there is something wrong. I can hear it in your voice. Do you want to tell me about it?"

Lena could hear Betty crying as she spoke. "We came home from getting the groceries yesterday and found that someone had broken into the house. The pretty little figurines that belonged to Miss Celia had been smashed against the walls, and some of the dishes too. Edward is on the porch and won't say a word to nobody."

"Did you call the sheriff?" Lena asked.

"Yeah, we called the sheriff, and he sent a boy here to look things over and take the report, but Edward would not say a word. I had to do all the talking for him. I'm afraid this might be too much for him."

Lena spoke rapidly. "I am coming over there to see if I can help. Don't worry, we'll take good care of him."

Lena slammed the phone down and reached for her purse. She wasted no time driving over to Edward's house. She knew he must be devastated from seeing the damage that had been done to Celia's things that could not be replaced. These were things that were sacred to him. And the thought of someone breaking into his home—the one place he found solace from the worries of the world was no longer safe to him.

Upon her arrival, she spotted Edward leaning against the tree by the river. He never turned nor glanced in her direction as she climbed from her car. Betty stood by the door and beckoned her to come inside. It was here Betty told her that he was refusing to eat and was still refusing to talk to anyone.

Lena ambled over to stand close by him. Edward never acknowledged her presence. She knew he was listening to every word she said, and still he never uttered a sound. His eyes were red-rimmed, as if he had been crying over the loss of the things he had held so precious in his heart for all these years. Lena pleaded with him to come inside and rest for just a while, if only to gather his thoughts. Still, he remained silent. Just as Lena turned to leave him, he reached for her hand. Holding it lightly within his own, he squeezed gently and walked away from her.

Through whispers and talking in low tones, the two women made a pact not to sleep. Their vigil over the old man was not to end until they were satisfied he would be all right. When the sun set low behind the mountains, he finally ventured onto the porch and sat heavily down upon his rocking chair. He sat alone in the darkness, humming an old gospel tune while smoking his pipe. They could see him clearly through the window, and he still never acknowledged their words to him.

Hours ticked by without a word parting his lips. Betty and Lena tried in vain to convince him to come inside. He sat staring vacantly across the yard toward the river, still slowly rocking, still smoking his worn pipe. A plate of food Betty sat beside his chair went untouched. Edward could not relieve his weary mind of the thoughts plaguing him. The sight of Celia's figurines lying shattered on the floor was all he could think of.

He felt as though he had failed her. He had failed to keep her things safe, and that was unforgivable in his eyes. Tears flowed down his cheeks because he knew someone had entered Celia's home and stolen her memories. They were precious times that could never be replaced. Edward's thoughts fairly screamed into the night. *They can never understand what they have done to me!*

He wanted to be alone in his misery. He needed the time to try to gain reasoning why this had happened to him. There was no reason in his mind for what had happened here. Being a strong man of what he felt to be a sound mind, he knew deep down the answer was not a reason but a question: why? Could someone dislike him so immensely they would destroy his home to get some kind of foolish revenge? He could think of no one he had wronged so greatly.

Betty slipped silently to the window and watched him. He was still as she had left him, never moving from his chair. Walking back to the kitchen, she poured a cup of coffee and sat down across from Lena. Neither spoke, and yet they shared the same thoughts. What was going to happen next? The night was too still. It felt as though a black cloud of misery hovered low over the once-cheerful house of Edward Caulfield.

This night was never-ending. The ticking of the clock was all that could be heard throughout the house. Each minute felt as though an eternity had passed them by. Lena glanced across the table to see Betty had laid her head down on her arms and had begun snoring gently. Rising silently from her chair, she made her way across the living room and sat close by the window. She wanted to be nearby should Edward need her. Within minutes, she also was sleeping soundly.

The sleep of the weary was long and deep, yet without reason, the slightest sound can awaken a person. Betty awoke from her slumber with a start. She had heard what seemed to be the sound of something scratching lightly on the wall next to her. Her thoughts instantly turned to Edward. Rising from her chair, she walked swiftly to the front door and opened it.

Stepping onto the porch, she saw that Edward still sat in the rocking chair smoking his pipe and staring toward the banks of the river. "You can't sit there forever, Edward. I suggest you come into the house and let me fix you some breakfast."

Edward ignored her and continued to rock.

Betty moved in front of him, blocking his view and forcing him to see and hear her. "I see this is what you want, but I will have my say. You cannot continue to act this way. You are not the first, or the last, to have someone come into your house and disturb your things. I am sorry they broke Miss Celia's figures. I know it hurt you deeply. The fact of the matter is, life does not begin and end with a few pieces of glass.

"If you think for two seconds Miss Celia would put up with the way you are behaving, you are wrong! You stand up like the man everybody knows you to be and get on with life. I will not stay here and worry myself to death because you want to act like a fool over this situation."

Edward looked up and spoke to Betty in low, clear voice. "I want you to sit down and shut your mouth. Then I will tell you exactly what is happening now."

Betty couldn't believe her ears. Dumbfounded, she sat on the steps and waited for him to tell her what he had to say. These words were out of character, and he had never ordered her to do anything during all their years together.

Edward took the time to repack his pipe before talking to her. He gazed steadily into Betty's face, unnerving her. "You mentioned Celia. I have no idea what her reaction to all this would be right now. I really don't think you do either. You let your temper get the best of you at the worst of times.

"Yesterday and all night last night I focused every thought toward what or who could have caused this. I had nothing to say because my mind was busy elsewhere. I feel like I had no time for nonsense. You handled the police report nicely, and I thank you for it. Did I get angry? You have no idea how angry I was when I saw what had happened in my house. I did not get angry over the porcelain figures being broken. I was hurt. My anger was focused on the theft of my memories of my wife. Each time I saw those figurines, they brought a little piece of my time with Celia back to me. If I see this right, this was not the actions of a child. I think it was of another nature I haven't figured out yet.

"I believe it was an adult in my house. The evidence of whoever was here is clear to me. A child would not take the time to steal bacon off the stovetop and eat it as he wanders through the house. Children always have a fear of getting caught when they are doing something wrong. This person feared nothing and went through the house looking at how I live. The sheriff's department did not take fingerprints. From what I saw on the doorjambs, those greasy fingerprints belonged to a grown man. The final straw for me was the back door. No child could have destroyed the screen door like that. He left in mighty big hurry.

"I will find out who was here, and I will punish him with my bare hands. The Bible says 'Vengeance is mine, sayeth the Lord,' but in the meantime I will be kicking his ass until the Lord can get here. That is all I have to say for now. If you want to fix breakfast, you can do it. I do feel a little bit hungry now."

Betty could find no words to say. Her face had reddened deeply, and she hardly believed the force of his words. Silently, she rose to her feet and went back into the house.

Lena awoke at the sound of the front door opening. "Is Edward all right?" she asked.

Betty shook her head. "I don't know if he is all right, but he sure is full of fire this morning."

Lena looked at her quizzically. Betty said nothing and continued on through the house to the kitchen. The sounds of

Betty getting things together in the kitchen came to Lena as she glanced through the window. Edward still sat in the chair, saying nothing while he stared out across the yard. Lena gathered her thoughts and headed for the kitchen. Betty turned slowly from her pile of pots and pans and glared at her. "Before you say a word, I will warn you he is not to be trifled with today. That is, unless you want your head handed to you. I already heard what he had to say, and I think we best leave him alone until he gets ready to be sociable."

Lena smiled. "At least he is talking now; that is a good sign."

"That would depend on how you look at it," Betty said as she prepared the dough for biscuits.

"Are you going to tell me what he said?" Lena asked.

Betty continued looking down at her fresh dough. "I think the subject should be left to him to talk about. He said so much, I believe I misjudged his brainpower as of late. He might have a weak moment here and there, but that old man ain't stupid by a long way. Today, his mind is as sharp as my old man's razor used to be. He won't sick yesterday, and he ain't today. Well, I just say leave him alone until he's ready for us."

Lena had little choice but to accept Betty's advice. If Edward was not ready to talk to them, it may not be wise for her to press him on his behavior. The heavy tread of boots on the bare wood caused them both to look toward the kitchen doorway.

Edward entered the kitchen and poured a cup of coffee. He gathered two large scoops of sugar and mixed it into the coffee with a tiny spoon next to the sink. Without any acknowledgement of their presence in the room, he pulled a chair from the table and sat down next to the window.

His silence seemed to dominate the room. He never asked for anything, nor did he offer any comments during the ladies' conversation. Edward finished his breakfast with a flourish and left the table.

As Edward walked from the room, Betty whispered to Lena across the table. "Do you see what I mean?"

Lena nodded her agreement with Betty's assessment of Edward. As the ladies continued their conversation, they were suddenly interrupted by the sound of an automobile engine. Jumping from their seats, they ran to the window, only to see Edward backing out of the driveway in Betty's car.

Lena shouted, "We have to stop him. He can't be driving!"

Betty shook her head. "You stop him. He has a license and he ain't done nothing illegal. Accordin' to his doctor, he ain't crazy. The only thing you can do is let go. From what I heard this morning on the porch, he might just need a little time to be by hisself."

Lena was nearly frantic with worry. She knew there was nothing she could do to keep him from driving. The only thing left for the both of them was to sit and wait for his return.

Chapter Nineteen

Driving was like riding a bicycle but much easier. It was pleasant to be driving the mountain roads again. He drove by farms and places he had not visited in many years. Some seemed to have never changed, while others were barely recognizable. If he had not known their locations, he would have doubted they were one in the same.

It was a beautiful day to just get away from everything and ramble through the countryside. Passing through the gorge, he saw tourists with kayaks tied to the roof of their cars and children playing in the water close to the shore. He smiled to himself as he saw families picnicking in the roadside rest areas, their smiles and laughter genuine. With the turn of each curve, the wonders of nature lay before him. He was feeling better about himself, the pain of his loss subsiding gradually.

Slowing almost to a crawl, Edward marveled once more at the sight of Bridal Veil Falls. He had brought Celia to see this wonder long before the state had ever paved the road and produced an area in which tourists could pull over and admire it. The sound of a car horn behind him caused him to regain speed. He wondered why people had deemed it necessary to rush through life and not enjoy what little time they had to be here among God's creations.

Two miles from the falls Edward pulled off the road and ventured down the side of the gorge to watch young men fly-fishing in the rushing waters. When he was younger, he had fished these same waters when they were teeming with large speckled trout. You didn't have to have a license, and the day was spent in pure enjoyment of the trout you produced for your supper.

The slight quiver in Edward's hands reminded him he was no longer capable of letting the fly line flow smoothly to its target in an effort to catch the big ones. He laughed softly and thought, *Maybe the day will come when I can try it again.*

Looking about him, he knew in his heart this was not to be, but it was a sin to give up hope. Edward sat and enjoyed the shade of the tree for another hour before returning to the car.

After starting the car, he rolled back onto the twisting mountain road and traveled a few more miles. He felt a deep hunger brewing inside of him and began to look for a place to get something to eat. Just ahead he recognized a sign for an old country store he used to frequent. He remembered it belonged to a German immigrant named Pritz. The old German used to make sandwiches to sell to people traveling these roads, and the food was well-known throughout the mountains. Pulling into the dirt drive, he realized the place still looked the same.

Edward was elated the old store was still in operation. Though the old German was long gone with the passage of time, the store had been taken over by his daughter and was still run in the traditional way of her father. There was a certain loneliness to the old store now. At one time you would wait in line for his food. His daughter stated it had not been the same in a very long time.

They stood and talked of her father while he ate his lunch and wished for some of the days past. She was delighted there was someone other than her family who still remembered the old German. Thanking her, Edward promised to return again and talk about her father in more detail.

Returning to the road, Edward saw a multitude of new houses built by strangers from other states for the sake of their vacations. It was good they would want to come here to enjoy a small piece of their lives. He knew their children would be able to see and hear things that would never be possible within the walls of large cities. Edward knew well the thrill of catching your first fish, hunting your first deer, or just watching your first sunrise from the top of a mountain. These were all things those children would never forget.

From the tree line, a large deer suddenly jumped into the path of Edward's car. He had to try to avoid the deer, and yet he knew not to jerk the wheel too suddenly. Barely missing the deer, he breathed a sigh of relief—but he was a second too late. The right rear tire could not gain traction in the fine gravel by the side of the road. The rear of the car spun sideways and refused to straighten when Edward turned his steering wheel in an effort to stop the slide. The guardrail ahead loomed menacingly as he fought for control. The front of the car slid almost to the guardrail, then suddenly dropped over the edge just before hitting the rail. The momentum was too great for the roadside shrubbery to slow him. Edward's eyes widened as he felt himself sliding over the embankment and heading for the bottom of the gorge.

The car rolled over twice as it crashed into the gorge, and then it landed on its wheels in the rushing waters of the rapids. The water was not filling the car as he thought was possible. Instead, the water rushed by at a force just great enough that he was unable to open the door to escape. An intense pain shot through him when he tried to move. He knew from a prior experience his ribs were broken. His entire body was in shock, and yet he knew he had to get himself to the bank of the river before he would be safe.

Gathering his thoughts, he looked about him. The car was a mangled mess with only a small space left for him to escape. His body was covered with glass, and he could see he was bleeding from several cuts.

Edward decided his best escape route would be the driver's-side window. It was the only opening left that seemed large enough to squeeze his body through. Grabbing the top edge of the door, he tried the pull himself into a position that enabled him to put his legs through the opening. The pain of movement was overwhelming. He knew if he was to try to escape headfirst he would drown.

Celia's sweet, hollow voice called to him. "Edward, can you hear me?"

Edward stopped. "I hear you, Celia. I must hurry, Celia, I don't have much time."

Celia's voice came from all around him. "Do not fear, Edward. I have come to you, and I will help you."

Edward was on the verge of tears from the pain he was experiencing. "How can you help me, Celia? I must get out of here before the car goes down the rapids."

Celia's gentle voice sent a calming effect through his mind. "Edward, you must listen. The time has come."

Edward was confused. The loss of blood was taking its toll on him. "Time? Time for what, Celia?"

Looking next to him, he saw her standing barely above the running waters, smiling. "The time has come for us to be together once again. Do not fear. There will be no pain, only the knowledge that we are never to be separated again for all eternity."

Celia held out her hands and grasped Edward's arms as he slid easily from the confines of the wreckage.

Above them witnesses watched as Edward slid from the window of the car and into the water. Edward never heard their cries to stay in the car or that help was on its way. Screams echoed through the gorge as Edward's body disappeared beneath the rushing water.

Betty tried hard to keep herself busy and not to worry about Edward's disappearance. She stuck to her routine of cleaning the house, while making excuses for being close to windows. Lena plainly saw her keeping a watch for the return of Edward and her car. At any other time, it may have been funny, but this was not the time.

Darkness was approaching, and dark, ominous clouds gathered above them. The newspaper had predicted a mild thunderstorm for the evening hours. It was their hope Edward would return before the rains began and lowered his visibility. The two of them decided to prepare supper in case of his return. He had always had a very good appetite, and they assumed that same appetite would make its appearance once he had time to evaluate everything and settle himself back into his routine.

Shortly after dark Betty spotted the headlights from a car coming up the path toward the house. With more than a little anxiety in her voice, she called out to Lena. "Lena, there is a car coming up the path and it's not mine. I would recognize the sound of my car anywhere, and that ain't it."

Lena ran to the window, trying to catch a good look at the strange vehicle. Within seconds, they were both able to recognize who had come to the house. "Betty, that's a police car."

Betty was close to strangling on her words. "I hope this does not have anything to do with Edward. Maybe he's here about the break-in the other day."

Both ladies headed for the door at the same time. Reaching the door, they opened it before the officer could raise his hand to knock.

Betty stepped back just enough to allow the officer to step inside the door. He stood with his hat in his hand and looked at Betty with eyes that told her this was not a social call.

"My goodness, they send the sheriff here at this time of night. What can I do for you? Edward ain't here, or he would talk to you hisself," Betty said.

The sheriff cleared his throat and cast his eyes away from Betty's face. "Betty, I need to talk to you, and you might want to take a seat before we start."

Betty's body tensed, but she kept her composure. "I think you have some bad news for me, so you might as well go ahead and spit it out."

The sheriff nodded. "A little after two o'clock this afternoon Edward lost control of his car and ended up at the bottom of the gorge. Witnesses said it wasn't his fault, but the accident was fatal. Within twenty minutes, we had Mountain Search and Rescue on the scene, but we were too late. With the rapids like they are, we found him down by the bridge. I am truly sorry, Betty."

Betty could not control herself and began to crumple to the floor. Lena and the sheriff grabbed her quickly and placed her in a chair. Her face was ashen, and they both feared she may not have been able to accept the news of Edward's death. Working with her, they were finally able to get her under control and talking with them.

The sheriff either could not or would not answer all of their questions. He fenced them like a true professional and guided them in the direction they needed to go to get the information they wanted. Lena walked the sheriff out to his car while trying to discuss what had happened.

"Can you at least tell me if he had a lot of injuries? I hate to think he had to suffer before he left us," she said.

The sheriff shoved his hands in his pockets and leaned back against the side of the car. "All I can tell you at this time is in a case such as this there are always injuries. To what extent will be in the coroner's report. You can get a copy of it from the courthouse one day next week. Personally, I would advise not getting a copy of the report for peace of mind. Sometimes it is better not to know than to make the pain worse than it already is.

"He should be at the funeral home for preparation day after tomorrow. North Carolina law states they have to do an autopsy. They will call you or be out to see you before then. We only have one funeral home here, and Mr. Parker will be the man you will be dealing with. Betty grew up with him, so he is no stranger to her. If I can do anything for you, just give me a call and I will be here as soon as possible."

Lena thanked him and watched as he started his car and rolled out of the driveway. She still could not believe Edward was dead. It was a nightmare with no end in sight. The feeling of loss she felt within her was indescribable. She knew her mind was denying all of the words that had been spoken concerning Edward. There were no tears, just a longing for the night to end and to wake up to see the old man smiling at her. She stood in the driveway looking at the stars above her, wondering what to do. The silence was as beautiful as it was frightening.

Lena trudged slowly back to the house, taking each step as if it were her last. Mounting the front steps, she tried to make as little noise as possible. When she reached the screen door, she hesitated slightly as thoughts of seeing Edward open this same door and enter the house flooded her mind.

Stepping just inside the door, she saw Betty sitting in Edward's chair, staring at everything and nothing at the same time. Lena crossed the room and reached for Betty's hand. They stared at each other for a brief moment before Betty spoke to her in a hushed tone. "Little girl, you have no idea how much that old man loved you. I heard him say you were the daughter he and Celia had always wanted. It was a fine thing to see the way his face would light up when you were here.

"He was the best friend I have ever known. I loved my husband dearly, but Edward was my friend. We went at each other all the time, but not in a bad way. He gave me anything I wanted, and I never took advantage of it. That is what friends do, you know. They never take advantage of you and accept you regardless of who you are.

"When other folks didn't care, he did. He did it for me, and I know in my heart he did it for you. You didn't have a lot of time with him, but I can promise you there was never a time when he didn't love you like his own. When you get old and your time is closer to the end, if you will remember Edward, I think you will find many lessons from him to help you live your days."

Betty laid her head back against the chair. "The Lord only knows how my heart is breaking right now. I don't worry about where I will go or who will be with me. I don't want to face the days of not hearing him walk through that door wanting his supper. The sound of his voice and the way he walked will all become memories that fade with the passage of time and weak minds. To me, that is the saddest thing of all."

Betty leaned forward and patted Lena's hand gently. "He walked the road with you as far as he could, and now it's your turn to do what you know is right. He told you what to do in his own way. If you were listening, I think you will find he was right. I made a bed for you today, and both of us need to go get some rest. We have a big day tomorrow."

Without another word, Betty rose from her chair and headed for the stairs. Lena sat and listened to her footsteps as she ascended the stairs. The house seemed so cold and empty. Lena hugged herself and curled up in Edward's chair by the window.

Slowly, the tears began to roll down her cheeks with the flood of memories. She could still see him packing his pipe and grinning as he teased Betty about some trivial instance in their life. Closing her eyes tightly, she could almost swear she could hear him laughing.

Unsure what to do with herself, Lena rose from Edward's chair and began walking through the house. She recalled the first time she was allowed to see the inside of the house. *Impressed* was not the word she would have chosen to describe what he had done here. It reached far beyond that. Without Edward, it was just a very pretty house, not a home filled with warmth and a love that was never to be forgotten.

A door just off the far wall of his library led to a small sun porch. Lena turned the handle and opened the door gently, trying not to make any sound that may awaken Betty from her sleep. The slate flooring was soothingly cool beneath her bare feet. She looked at the flowers and green plants Betty had placed in the room to try to make it feel more comfortable to those who came to visit. Edward would come here on rainy days and read from one of his many books in his library. Lena reached down and picked up a book Edward had left on the day bed. The cover was worn and the volume had seen its pages turned many times over the years. It was an anthology of poetry. There were almost a dozen authors listed in the index, and a select few had check marks placed beside them. It was Lena's best guess that these were placed here by a woman, judging from the sweep of the tails of the markings. Opening the book, she discovered a bookmark made of silk marking a particular verse. It was the "Tintern Abbey" by William Wordsworth.

Reading the passages before her, she could feel the power of the words written here. It gave her a greater understanding of the man Edward truly was and why he lived his life in search of himself. If indeed these were also the words he lived by, written by someone else, it would explain why he was very much a stranger to all who thought they knew him.

Lena closed the book slowly and looked about the small room. It was enclosed with glass from floor to ceiling. There was nothing you could not see from here, including the star-filled sky above. The room brought an inner peace that was difficult to find anywhere. She wondered if this room was of his design or Celia's. Whoever it was knew what they wanted, and the thoughts were conveyed very clearly for those who would see.

Lena lay down on the day bed, clutching the worn book to her chest. Her last thoughts before drifting off to sleep were of the amazing view of the stars above her.

Betty rose from her bed early the following morning. Sleep evaded her at every turn. She was also aware the day would be filled with people stopping by to convey their condolences. It was the hardest part of losing anyone close to you. Nobody really understands how you feel, and yet it is always brought to your attention before they leave you. She understood they all meant well, but still, in the back of her mind she wished they would all go away.

Betty did not see Lena in her room and decided to look into some of the other rooms before going to prepare breakfast. She found her on the day bed in the sun room and decided to let her sleep.

Walking into the kitchen, she started removing her frying pans and mixing bowl from the cabinets. It suddenly struck her there was no longer a true reason for her to cook anything. The habit of having Edward's breakfast ready every morning was deeply ingrained, and it would be a hard habit to break. Placing the pans back into the cupboard, she made a fresh pot of coffee and sat down at the table, staring out of the window.

Slowly she lifted her head and turned toward the back door. On the coat hook by the pantry door, she saw Edward's battered old brown fedora he had worn when he worked in the yard. She could almost see his crooked grin as he would pull the hat from his head and throw it across the room to land on the sofa. There was never a time when she had not scolded him for not hanging up his hat. He would just laugh and head for the cookie jar.

Just before lunch, Kate's Florist came to the house and placed a wreath on the front door. Betty knew she had not had the time to order flowers, and Lena had gone back to the cabin to prepare herself for the people who would stop by Edward's house. Betty asked the lady who had ordered the flowers so she would know if there would be a bill she needed to pay. The lady shook her head and told her the flowers were from Kate and her family.

From that moment, a slow parade of friends and acquaintances came and went throughout the day and well into the evening. Everyone brought food or flowers, trying to ease the pain of losing a loved one. Mr. Parker from the funeral home came to her early in the afternoon to make the arrangements for Edward's final resting place.

Betty listened to everything he had to say and nodded her agreement to almost everything. "Mr. Parker, Edward gave me a paper I was supposed to give to you if anything should ever happen to him. I am sure the other arrangements you suggested will be fine, but I can tell you now he wanted to spend his eternal rest up on the hill here in back of the house next to Celia."

Mr. Parker read over the paper she had given him and nodded. "I will see to it that everything is done as he wanted it to be. I will give you a call this afternoon to let you know when we will have him ready for visitation."

Betty simply nodded and followed him to the door. She could not find any more words to convey how she felt or just to be polite to the man who had come to help her. She patted him gently on the shoulder and turned away.

Chapter Twenty

The house seemed to sigh, as if it knew Edward was no longer here. Edward's lawyer and Dr. Early came to visit and pay their respects. They were aware Betty was all the family Edward had as far as anyone was concerned, and she knew his personal business almost as much as he had.

The clock in the hallway chimed eight as the last of the mourners left the old house by the river. Dr. Early and Edward's lawyer stayed behind, knowing they needed to speak with Lena and Betty alone.

Once back in the kitchen, Betty poured each a cup of fresh coffee and shared a coconut cake brought to them by Buck Queen. He told them it was from all of his men who had known and liked Mr. Caulfield. Betty knew if Edward were able, he would have thanked them for their kindness.

Edward's lawyer drew in a slow breath and began. "Betty, you are already aware of what Edward had in his will for you, and we can get all of that done as soon as you feel you are ready. Lena, you are the reason I stayed until the others had gone. Edward was a good man. More than some people will ever know. He was a good friend to me when I needed it, and I have never forgotten what he did for me. What I am going to tell you now cannot be told to anyone.

"Edward came to my office close to two weeks ago and added a codicil to his will. When he told me the importance of his change, I had the clerk of the court take care of it immediately after he left my office."

Lena drew in a deep breath. "What has that got to do with me?"

"Edward has placed it in his will that you are to receive the remainder of his estate with conditions. The conditions exist until you are ready or you sign a document stating you cannot accept the conditions of the will," he said.

Lena sat erect in her chair. "What are these conditions? I have never asked for anything from Edward, and I have no idea why he would do this."

"Edward explained to me why he was doing this, and I considered it to be not only a generous gesture but it would be beneficial to your future. As far as the conditions are concerned, you would have to divorce your husband to receive the inheritance and you will have to reside here in this house. The house can never be sold or any of the property.

"This house, along with the land and a considerable sum of money, would be yours. You can do with it as you please. But they are the conditions and cannot be negotiated," he stated flatly.

Lena sat in shock of this sudden news. It took a few minutes for her to absorb what she had been told. "I have already told Edward how I feel about divorcing my husband. Conditions would have to drastically change for me to go against my words to him."

The lawyer nodded slowly. "Yes, Edward informed me of your feelings toward divorce from your husband. The offer is still in your court and will remain so until I hear something different from you." Slowly he rose from his seat and smiled gently. "Think about it, Lena, and in the meantime you already have the invitation to stay here as long as you desire. Ladies, I bid you good night, and I will see you again at Edward's funeral."

Betty walked to the door with Dr. Early and the lawyer. Stepping onto the porch, she spoke to them in a low tone. "I knew Edward was up to something, I am just happy it was for the little girl's benefit."

Both men just smiled and walked gingerly down the steps and out to their cars.

Betty reentered the house and headed for the kitchen. To her surprise, Lena was no longer there. Listening carefully, she could hear her upstairs in the guest room above her. Chuckling to herself, she felt as though she could almost dance with the thought Lena may get rid of the pond scum she had married. Her decision either way would not change the fact Lena had a friend in her for life.

Betty turned and saw Lena coming down the stairs with a small clothing bag in her hand. "Are you leaving now?" Betty asked.

Lena stepped lightly to the bottom of the stairs and nodded. "I hope you don't mind, but I feel like I need to go back to the cabin and think about what Edward's lawyer said to me. I will be back again when we go to the funeral."

Betty nodded. "I guess it is a lot to think about. Edward was a wise man in many ways—just a thought you may want to consider. I expect he saw some things in your story you couldn't see."

Lena stared blankly at Betty for a few seconds. Without another word, Betty turned and disappeared beyond the doorway. The sun would soon be setting behind the mountains. The sight of such a fine evening made her stop and think about the sadness we never seem to notice that can be hidden within.

Once she was on the highway headed for the cabin, everything seemed like just another evening as she passed people still mowing lawns or washing cars. The sights rolled by almost in slow motion. She had become preoccupied with her thoughts and nearly missed the road she needed to turn onto to reach her mountain home.

Within minutes she was rounding the sharp turn at the top of the mountain, leading her through a canopy of trees. From this point she could easily see her driveway and noticed Gerald's car sitting close to the garage door. His timing was a curiosity. Shaking her head in mild disgust, she pulled in beside his car and shut down the engine.

She sat looking at the cabin, shaking her head and tapping the steering wheel with her finger. The soft clink of her wedding band hitting the wheel just served to worsen her mood. Lena unbuckled her seat belt and bolted from the car, leaving her overnight bag still in the trunk.

As she glanced about her, everything seemed normal as she reached for the front doorknob. Suddenly the door opened and Lena drew back, gasping. Gerald stood before her smiling and reached to draw her near to him. Lena stepped back quickly and found herself pinned to the post supporting the front porch. "Gerald, what happened to you?"

Gerald looked at her questioningly. "I have no idea what you are talking about. I put on a few pounds, but other than that, it's still me."

Lena barely recognized the man before her. His hair was no longer full and beautiful; it lay on his skull in tufts not unlike a dog with mange. His blotched skin hung in folds among the fat hanging from his now-huge jowls. The thought of touching him was revolting. When he spoke, his mouth reeked like the mouth of something that had been eating rotten meat.

Lena stayed where she was, trying not to look into his face. "Gerald, if you don't mind, I want to go in the house and get a shower. It's been a long day already."

Gerald sneered, "This is not much of a welcome for your husband. I guess you didn't expect me to come here at all. You act as though I am a stranger who has invaded your space."

Lena charged by him and entered the living room, keeping her distance from him. "Why are you here?"

Gerald shoved his hands deep into his pockets and cocked his head. "I thought you may want your husband by your side at a time like this."

"Meaning what, Gerald?"

Gerald almost sneered. "Meaning you just lost your friend and I thought we would attend his funeral together. You know, pay our respects. I am sure Edward would appreciate it."

Lena's eyes flared. "What would you know about Edward Caulfield besides what your weak-minded little rats have told you? It's really strange you knew about his death so fast."

Gerald moved to a place by the window and looked out over the mountains. "I am a man who must know what is going on in his life and the lives of those close to him. That includes my wife. My employees informed me right away—I would say just about an hour after the accident. I am sure it was an accident."

Lena scowled. "Where is Gena?"

Gerald fingered the shade of the lamp by the sofa as he spoke. "I sent her on vacation so I could have some time alone with my wife during her time of grief. It isn't every day you lose a friend as close as Edward. Not to worry, all expenses were paid and she won't have to worry about anything."

Lena turned and walked into the kitchen. Opening the refrigerator, she reached inside and grabbed a cold soda. She slammed the door and looked directly at Gerald. "Yes, I am sure she will be taken care of at my father's expense. That *is* how it works, isn't it, Gerald?"

Gerald stepped forward. The look upon his face was as if he wanted to strike her. "I took care of her expenses out of our account. You never went without because of me, that's for sure."

Lena laughed heartily. "So true, Gerald. But unlike your playmates, I am very low maintenance. Tell me, Gerald—you never cared before—what really brought you here now besides a slice of paranoia?"

Gerald sat heavily in a chair next to the sliding doors that led to the deck. The chair nearly buckled beneath his weight. "Okay, you want it? You'll find out soon enough. You and Caulfield were so close that I am sure he left you a little something in his will. Don't look so surprised. I have only acquired a portion of the will, but it was enough. That house and property will sell for a fortune—all that unique trim work, not to mention a view unequaled anywhere around here. I know a few developers who will pay handsomely for that property. You are my wife, and that entitles me to half of anything you have. It is only fitting I should pay my respects to the man who made me truly rich."

Lena exploded. "It was you! You son of a bitch, you were the one who broke into Edward's house. That is the only way you could have known what the inside of his house looks like. You have no idea what you did to that old man, and if you think for two seconds you will ever be forgiven for it, you are dead wrong!"

Gerald just looked at her, saying nothing and everything at the same time.

Lena slung the can of soda at Gerald, barely missing his head.

Gerald rose from his chair. "I think it's time you came home and forgot this nonsense of staying here among the country boys. My wife has a place in society and obligations that must be met to keep her standard of living, if you get my drift.

"Tomorrow we will spend some time together, and I will tell you exactly what is going to happen. Trust me, you have no choice in the matter. The funeral for your friend will be on Friday at two o'clock. You and I will be there like the loving couple we are. When we return home, you can close up this place and we will go back to Richmond."

Lena narrowed her eyes. "I am going to the funeral, and that is a fact. Am I going with you? I will be there with you when hell freezes over. You get whatever is crawling up your backside to lie still long enough for you to find out who will be doing what. I can guarantee after what you did to me and Edward, I will see to it your life is going to be anything but pleasant."

Gerald laughed. "You are out of your league, little girl. I have been dealing with men of true power long enough to know people like you do not stand a chance against people like me. I have the money and I have the power. Do you still think you can win this game?"

"You see this as a game? Gerald, these are people's lives you are dealing with. It is anything but a game. Where is your dignity? Where is your sense of decency? Sometimes I believe you never had either of those virtues."

Gerald curled his lips and glared at her. "I would suggest you gain control of yourself and be very careful about what you say to me."

Lena leaned forward with her sexiest smile and tugged at the knot in his tie playfully. "Gerald, I have already won, and you were too blind to see it." She suddenly pushed hard and caught Gerald off balance. With a sudden twist, she bolted for her bedroom and locked the door behind her.

Wasting little time, she opened the drawer of the nightstand and removed a small black book. The book contained every phone number of importance to her. It was a habit of keeping separate phone books in case of emergencies that her father had taught her.

Picking up the phone, Lena dialed the number of Charles Messer. She needed him desperately and prayed he would answer her call. On the second ring, she heard the audible click of the receiver being raised. Lena did not give him any time to say as much as hello. "Don't say a word, just listen. Gerald is in the house, and I have no idea if he is listening on the other line.

"I am sure he is the man who broke into Edward's house the other night. You said you had all the papers you needed to do what you do. Now is the time. I want you to get those to the right people tonight. *The right people, you understand?* Edward's funeral is at two o'clock Friday. I'll call you again after it's over. If you understand what I said, just hang up the phone and go as quickly as possible!"

Barely had she finished speaking when she heard the audible click of the connection being broken.

Charles was as surprised as he was elated by her call. One of the things he enjoyed most in life was to see the downfall of arrogant pigs like Gerald Leicester. Gloating, he gathered all of the materials out of his safe and left immediately for Lena's father's house. Who better to reap the rewards of his information than the man Gerald was burying one check at a time?

Within twenty minutes, Charles was getting out of car and approaching the front door of Lena's father's home. Charles rang the doorbell, hoping he did not sound impatient. On the third ringing of the bell, the senator's servant came to the door. "May I help you, sir?" he asked.

Charles took a small step forward, keeping his voice to a minimum, and handed the servant his card. "Would you tell the senator that Charles Messer needs to speak with him on a matter of great importance? His daughter sent me here with these papers for him." Charles tapped his briefcase to let the man know where the papers were.

The servant stood straight and asked if Charles would wait in the foyer. "I will see if the senator is available to see you at this time, sir."

The servant vanished from sight and reappeared within a very short time, accompanied by the senator. "Hello, Charles. Has something happened to my daughter?"

Charles glanced at the servant and spoke evenly. "Sir, I have some papers of great importance for you that your daughter has asked me to make sure you get tonight. I can explain them all to you, but I think you may want to do this in the privacy of your office."

The senator glanced at his servant, and said, "Very well, you are dismissed, and you can come this way, Charles. I must say, you have my undivided attention already." Entering the office, the senator offered Charles a seat across from his massive cherry-wood desk.

"It is good to see you again, Charles. I must say, I never see you anymore unless we are crossing paths on business."

Charles grimaced. "I wish this could be a social call, sir. What I have here is not only of importance but it will require your pull as a senator to get the ball rolling really fast." Reaching into his briefcase, he pulled the dossier from it and placed it on the desk before the senator. "If you will notice, sir, it carries the name of one Gerald Leicester."

The senator picked up the dossier and then began to read. Slowly, he lowered the papers to the top of the desk and looked Charles straight into his eyes. "Tell me where you received this information, Charles."

Charles cleared his throat as he repositioned himself in the high-backed leather chair. "Lena came to me and asked for an investigation. It would seem she knew what he was doing and to whom. She wasn't able to stop the deeds, but she wanted full knowledge of his actions so she could bring them to your attention. She had no desire for you to wake up one morning and find your hard work had been for nothing. According to our investigation, you will find his latest venture caused those deaths with the faulty steel. All the proof is there for you, including legal wiretaps of his office, approved by the attorney general, concerning his transactions with questionable people in Dubai. The names as well as all pertinent information concerning everyone involved are indexed for you. All sources are named and indexed.

"My legal department has assured me that, with what you see before you, there is no reason why this man cannot be charged with his crimes immediately. Everything you will need for his immediate arrest is in the file. The file contains enough information for this young man to never see daylight again in our lifetime. You will find a warrant for his arrest signed by Judge Drew, and it only requires your signature for immediate arrest on federal and state charges. May I add, sir, you may find his secretary of interest also. As I said, Lena requested this to be brought to your attention tonight."

The senator sat back, reading through the dossier with amazement. With amazement came anger, and then he reached for the phone. Before dialing, he looked at Charles. "I understand Gerald is at the cabin now. He left for somebody's funeral or other."

Charles nodded. "That is correct, sir. Lena's friend, Mr. Edward Caulfield, passed away, and the funeral is at two o'clock Friday."

"I understand. Do you know where the service will be held?"

Charles reached into his pocket and removed a small book from his pocket. "Service will be held at Barton's Creek Church in North Carolina, with the burial behind his house after the service. He wanted to be buried next to his wife on top of the mountain."

With the phone still in his hand, he smiled at Charles. "I think I can make this memorial one Gerald will remember for years to come. Please find some way of letting Lena know I will be attending her friend's funeral."

Still smiling, he dialed a number hidden from Charles. "Good evening, may I speak with David, please?"

Without a word, Charles dismissed himself and left the senator's home with a broad smile upon his lips.

Chapter Twenty-One

Lena was afraid to sleep, not knowing if Gerald would try to harm her. Before the sun first appeared over the mountains, she readied herself and slipped quietly out through the sliding doors leading to the sun deck. She raced for her car, praying Gerald would not awaken and try to stop her. Closing her car door as quietly as she possibly could, Lena shoved the gearshift into neutral and glided silently out of sight of the house. Once she felt she had gone far enough, she started the engine and raced for Edward's house.

Betty was still awake when Lena came through the door. She was surprised at her early arrival. One look at her face and Betty knew something had happened. "You are here too early. My best guess is something happened after you left here. Do you want to talk about it?"

Lena sighed heavily and poured two cups of coffee. "When I got back to the cabin, Gerald was there. He said he came for the funeral. Smart mouth said he wanted to pay his respects. He slipped up when he was talking, and just as good as told me he was the one who broke into the house before Edward died.

"I locked my bedroom door so he couldn't get in. Soon as it was light enough, I slipped out of the house when the sun was coming up. But I tell you, I know him too well; he will be here today."

Betty frowned. "I can arrange it so he cain't come on the property unless you approve of it."

Lena flopped her head down on the kitchen table. Her voice sounding muffled. "With a man like that, he will find a way to make everybody miserable. I say we wait and see what happens. Maybe he'll make a fool out of himself and the sheriff will take care of it for us."

"Okay, before the funeral we'll go down the street and get you a dress to wear. I need shoes anyway, so it ain't a problem. Besides, you have a car and I don't have a ride right this minute." Betty's small joke served to lighten the mood for a few minutes, and both had a good laugh to start the day.

Before they had finished laughing, the phone in the living room started to ring. Lena glanced toward the living room. "I'll answer it, Betty. I have the feeling His Highness has awakened and found me missing." Lena picked up the phone. "Hello?"

The voice on the other end of the line was not familiar. "May I speak with Lena Leicester, please?"

Lena was confused. Nobody except Gerald and Charles knew she was here. Yet the voice was that of a stranger. "This is she, how may I help you?"

The stranger cleared his throat and excused himself for doing so. "My name is David Wise with the United States Marshal's office. I am an old friend of your father. I am calling on his behalf to send his condolences to the family of Edward Caulfield and to notify you he will be in attendance for the service today. He has also asked me to tell you that he wanted to be with you in your time of sorrow. Please know he would have called you himself, but he is currently en route to be with you."

Lena was shocked beyond belief. "I appreciate your call, David, and I will eagerly await his arrival. Will he be coming to the house or the church?"

David paused. "Your father will be coming to the house for the graveside service. Local law enforcement has been notified, so please don't be alarmed when you see them."

It was a feeling she thought had been dead for years. Her father was aware of her loss and was making an effort to be with her. Lena thanked the marshal and placed the phone gently back into the cradle. Turning in her tracks, as if in a dream, Lena stood smiling broadly at Betty. "My father is coming to be with us today, Betty. It is something I never thought would happen."

Betty flushed. "Your daddy, the senator, is coming here?"

"Yes, he is. He is already on his way," Lena said.

"I reckon I best pick out my best dress and put another chicken on the stove. I know he'll bring folks with him, and I don't want them to go away hungry. Edward would come back and skin me if I did. Does your daddy like deviled eggs?"

"Betty, don't make a fuss over him. I want you to treat him just like you do me, okay?"

"Little girl, your daddy is an important man, and we want to make a good impression on him. I don't want him to go back to Washington tellin' folks we didn't feed him right."

Lena raised her hands in self-defense. "Okay, you win, but he won't be here long, I don't think. He will probably have to get back as soon as possible."

Betty was excited. She had never met a senator before. There was a notable thing about Betty that few realized. Whenever she became excited, she developed a little hop in her walk. Due to her being a little on the plump side, her excitement seemed to accentuate the hop in her walk. Lena watched her strut back to the kitchen whistling merrily. It was everything she could do to control her laughter.

The hands of time stood still for no one, and the morning slipped away from them almost before they knew it. When Betty and Lena arrived at the church, there was already a large crowd of mourners to meet them. They stood in the churchyard greeting the many friends of Edward who came to bid him a last farewell. Lena knew Edward was well-known here in this town, and yet she was astounded at the number of people who came to see him one last time.

Betty had provided him with his best suit and tie, and she reminded the funeral home to make sure he had a yellow rose in his lapel. She told them he had to look his best when he saw Celia again. They smiled and assured her that Edward would have nothing but the best they had to offer.

Through the singing of psalms and the gentle words of friends and the minister, Betty stood fast and held a silent prayer for her best friend. The end of the service brought the minister to her, and he bent over to whisper words of the Lord and of encouragement in an effort to heal her heart. When the casket was closed, Betty could no longer hold back the flood of tears and the heartbreak she felt deep within.

Lena guided her from her seat and walked her gently back to a limousine waiting for them, letting her know she would never be alone. The silence of the ride home was unsettling.

Edward's body was to be taken from the house to the burial site in the back of the same carriage he had bought for Celia. Neighbors had cleaned and polished it so it shone like the sun.

The mourners made their way up the hill to the burial site and waited for the minister and Edward to arrive. A deputy in his best uniform led the carriage up the hill and stopped close by Edward's grave. Those who chose to see his final resting place found themselves surrounding the gravesite, waiting for the minister's final prayer. At the end of the minister's prayer, a lone voice echoed through the hills, singing sweetly.

Lena dreaded every second. The loss of Edward was far greater than she thought it would be. It was an unsettling moment when Gerald made his presence known and came to stand beside of her. He was one of the last to arrive. Gerald stood boldly by Lena, holding her arm in mock support of her. He was mildly surprised to see her father standing close by the end of the casket and staring at the both of them. Lena's father saw Lena flinch just barely on several occasions when Gerald touched her.

The service ended with the closing notes of a psalm. The band of people slowly started walking back down the hill as the final notes of the singer's song wafted away down the mountainside.

Gerald turned to walk with them and suddenly found himself looking into the face of the county sheriff. "Are you Gerald Leicester?"

Gerald stood erect with a look of disdain on his face. "I am. What is the problem?"

The sheriff smiled. "There are some gentlemen waiting to speak with you."

Gerald looked around and saw Lena's father headed toward them with two very large men in black suits and dark glasses, accompanied by Edward's lawyer and Dr. Early. Behind them walked an old Indian with his hat pulled low over his eyes. The two men in dark suits stood menacingly directly in front of Gerald. "Gerald Leicester, we are with the U.S. Marshals office and we have a warrant for your arrest. I would advise you not to resist. Place your hands behind your back, and this gentleman will give you some new jewelry." The marshal began to read him his rights as he placed the handcuffs on him.

Gerald stammered, "W-w-what the hell is going on here?"

Lena's father stood close to him. "Gerald, you are being charged, just for starters, with manslaughter, fraud, embezzlement, and conspiracy against the United States government. As I said, that is just a start. You will be leaving us for a very long time. This is one time when my wife can't get you out of what you have done. I almost forgot to tell you: you are also being held with no chance of bond in a federal facility. As far as legal advice is concerned, you will have to get a court-appointed attorney for representation. At ten a.m. this morning, the court placed an order to seize all of your assets."

The old Indian walked close by and looked at Gerald from between the two marshals. "Edward was right; you look better this way." Without another word, he turned and continued down the hill. The small band of men stared off after him, wondering about his statement.

The sheriff stepped forward and tucked a warrant into Gerald's coat pocket. "Mr. Leicester, just in case you can wheedle out of the other charges, this is a warrant for your arrest in my county. I have a man in my jail who will swear you paid him to break into one of the local lawyers' office. I want to congratulate you—that is another felony to chew on. I have been an officer of the law for close to twenty-six years, and I have never had the opportunity to arrest somebody at a funeral."

Lena and Betty could hardly believe their ears. Gerald whined like a lost child as the marshals led him back down the hill. The sheriff apologized if the arrest caused any embarrassment or discomfort during this time. Lena laughed. "It made my day, Sheriff. I do have a question for you though."

"Yes, how can I help?"

"Who was that old Indian who stopped earlier? And one more thing, if you please. Ask Edward's lawyer to come and see me."

"I certainly will. As for the Indian, I wouldn't pay a lot of attention to him. Some say he is a witch, and I think he believes it."

Lena giggled like a schoolgirl, and Betty hung on to her arm, laughing hard. Betty whispered in Lena's ear. "Now I know what Edward meant when he said I would know what he done to Gerald."

Lena's father stepped forward and introduced himself. With a smile, he asked, "Would you ladies like to have dinner with me tonight?"

Betty grabbed him by the arm. "Yes, I would, but I'll be the one doin' the cookin'."

The rest of the evening was like a dream for Betty. She had met and talked with a senator. For her it was the closest thing ta movie star she would ever know. Lena took some pictures for her, and she could never remember seeing her father laugh as much as he did that evening.

Excusing herself, Lena needed some time alone. The feelings of loss and loneliness she would never be able to describe had embraced her. She wanted to walk down the gravel path and remember her friend and the good times they had. The memories of sitting by the river and talking while sharing a lunch came back, as though Edward had never left.

The sun had disappeared behind the mountains, and the light of the moon caressed the landscape about her. She stopped and stood by the river where Edward had proposed to Celia so many years before. Looking up the river into the mist, she was suddenly held spellbound by the sight before her. The spirits of Edward and Celia were waltzing on the misty waters of the Nantahala. As the apparitions began to fade, Lena smiled and walked quietly away.

Some swear there are the ghosts of a man and woman who dance upon the misty waters of the Nantahala even today when the moon is full and the flowers are in bloom. Those who knew Edward Caulfield will only smile and tell you "true love never dies," and just leave it at that.

Author Biography

Micheal, born in 1953, is an American author. His writing genres include Fiction, Horror, Thriller, and Paranormal. Micheal has been writing for several years. In the past he concentrated on Romantic Poetry.

In recent years he has focused on writing Fiction and Paranormal stories. His book titled *Ghosts of the North Carolina Shores* has been published by Schiffer Publishing Ltd. Micheal also published the e-book *The Black Witch*, which is the first of a series on Amazon and Barnes and Noble. Micheal has over thirty years of investigating and collecting stories of the paranormal. He is the lead investigator for the Smokey Mountain Ghost Trackers of Western North Carolina.

(www.facebook.com/SmokeyMtnGhostTrackers).

He served his country as a United States Marine during Vietnam. He is a native North Carolinian, and he lived in the Chicago area in the past and furthered his education there. He served the community as an Emergency Medical Technician while living there. Micheal currently resides in the mountains of North Carolina along with his wife and his boxer he fondly calls Dee Dee.

Made in the USA
Las Vegas, NV
04 November 2021